What Is Lonergan Up to in *INSIGHT*?

A Primer

Terry J. Tekippe

A Michael Glazier Book
THE LITURGICAL PRESS
Collegeville, Minnesota

Cover design by David Manahan, O.S.B.

A Michael Glazier Book published by The Liturgical Press

1   2   3   4   5   6   7   8

Library of Congress Cataloging-in-Publication Data

Tekippe, Terry J.
    What is Lonergan up to in Insight? : a primer / Terry J. Tekippe.
        p.   cm.
    "A Michael Glazier book"—T.p.
    Includes bibliographical references (p.).
    ISBN 0-8146-5782-6
    1. Lonergan, Bernard J. F.   Insight.   2. Knowledge, Theory of.
I. Title.
BD161.L613T45   1996
121—dc20   96-4761
                                                      CIP

Contents

Preface

Bernard Lonergan's *Insight: A Study of Human Understanding* is one of the most brilliant books of the twentieth century. It is also one of the most difficult. Innumerable readers have been daunted by its challenges, and still more have been warned away by its reputation. What has been needed is a book to introduce, on an accessible level, the leading ideas of Lonergan's massive work. This book will, I hope, fill that need.

Neither a commentary, a summary, nor a substitute for *Insight* is intended, but an easier approach to the book itself. Except in manner of presentation, no originality is claimed for the ideas expressed; indeed, the intention has been to avoid originality, and to communicate faithfully Lonergan's own leading inspirations. Any such re-presentation, however, is inevitably also an interpretation, and readers and Lonergan scholars will have to judge whether its intention of fidelity to Lonergan's profound thought is in fact fulfilled.

I am grateful and happy to acknowledge the provision by Archbishop Francis B. Schulte and Notre Dame Seminary in New Orleans of the sabbatical time for this writing. Deep gratitude is also due to Rev. Joseph Flanagan, S.J.—who has genially presided over the Philosophy Department at Boston College for so many years—for arranging the Lonergan Fellowship in the spring semester of 1993, with the incomparable human and library resources it affords. I also fondly remember the other Fellows, Rev. Chris Spalatin, S.J., and especially Dr. Andrew Beards, who was unfailingly encouraging on this project.

1

The Myth of the Cave

In the seventh book of the *Republic*, Plato presents one of the most famous of the myths that adorn his dialogues. This story of the cave-dwellers has everything to do with the endeavor of this work—so much so, in fact, that it will be impossible to explain it all at once. Plato's myth is almost a compendium of the whole project at hand; accordingly, certain directions will be taken from it immediately, and then the pregnant story will be returned to from time to time. But now, let Socrates speak for himself:

> Next, said I, compare our nature in respect of education and its lack to such an experience as this. Picture men dwelling in a sort of subterranean cavern with a long entrance open to the light on its entire width. Conceive them as having their legs and necks fettered from childhood, so that they remain in the same spot, able to look forward only, and prevented by the fetters from turning their heads. Picture further the light from a fire burning higher up and at a distance behind them, and between the fire and the prisoners and above them a road along which a low wall has been built, as the exhibitors of puppet shows have partitions before the men themselves, above which they show the puppets.
>
> All that I see, he said.
>
> See also, then, men carrying past the wall implements of all kinds that rise above the wall, and human images and shapes of animals as well, wrought in stone and wood and every material, some of these bearers presumably speaking and others silent.
>
> A strange image you speak of, he said, and strange prisoners.
>
> Like to us, I said. For, to begin with, tell me do you think that these men would have seen anything of themselves or of one another

except the shadows cast from the fire on the wall of the cave that fronted them?

How could they, he said, if they were compelled to hold their heads unmoved through life?

And again, would not the same be true of the objects carried past them?

Surely.

If then they were able to talk to one another, do you not think they would suppose that in naming the things that they saw they were naming the passing objects?

Necessarily.

And if their prison had an echo from the wall opposite them, when one of the passers-by uttered a sound, do you think that they would suppose anything else than the passing shadow to be the speaker?

By Zeus, I do not, said he.

Then in every way such prisoners would deem reality to be nothing else than the shadows of the artificial objects.

Quite inevitably, he said.

Consider, then, what would be the manner of the release and healing from these bonds and this folly if in the course of nature something of this sort should happen to them. When one was freed from his fetters and compelled to stand up suddenly and turn his head around and walk and to lift up his eyes to the light, and in doing all this felt pain and, because of the dazzle and glitter of the light, was unable to discern the objects whose shadows he formerly saw, what do you suppose would be his answer if someone told him that what he had seen before was all a cheat and an illusion, but that now, being nearer to reality and turned toward more real things, he saw more truly? And if also one should point out to him each of the passing objects and constrain him by questions to say what it is, do you not think that he would be at a loss and that he would regard what he formerly saw as more real than the things now pointed out to him?

Far more real, he said.

And if he were compelled to look up at the light itself, would not that pain his eyes, and would he not turn away and flee to those things which he is able to discern and regard them as in very deed more clear and exact than the objects pointed out?

It is so, he said.

And if, said I, someone should drag him thence by force up the ascent which is rough and steep, and not let him go before he had drawn him out into the light of the sun, do you not think that he would find it painful to be so haled along, and would chafe at it, and when he came out into the light, that his eyes would be filled with its beams so that he would not be able to see even one of the things that we call real?

Why, no, not immediately, he said.

Then there would be need of habituation, I take it, to enable him to see the things higher up. And at first he would most easily discern the shadows and, after that, the likenesses or reflections in water of men and other things, and later, the things themselves, and from those he would go on to contemplate the appearances in the heavens and heaven itself, more easily by night, looking at the light of the stars and the moon, than by day the sun and the sun's light.

Of course.

And so, finally, I suppose he would be able to look upon the sun itself and see its true nature, not by reflections in water or phantasms of it in an alien setting, but in and by itself in its own place.

Necessarily, he said.

And at this point he would infer and conclude that this it is that provides the seasons and the courses of the year and presides over all things in the visible region, and is in some sort the cause of all these things that they had seen.

Obviously, he said, that would be the next step.

Well then, if he recalled to mind his first habitation and what passed for wisdom there, and his fellow bondsmen, do you not think that he would count himself happy in the change and pity them?

He would indeed.

And if there had been honors and commendations among them which they bestowed on one another and prizes for the man who is quickest to make out the shadows as they pass and best able to remember their customary precedences, sequences, and coexistences, and so most successful at guessing at what was to come, do you think he would be very keen about such rewards, and that he would envy and emulate those who were honored by these prisoners and lorded it among them, or that he would feel with Homer and greatly prefer while living on earth to be serf of another, a landless man, and endure anything rather than opine with them and live that life?

Yes, he said, I think that he would choose to endure anything rather than such a life.

And consider this also, said I. If such a one should go down again and take his old place would he not get his eyes full of darkness, thus suddenly coming out of the sunlight?

He would indeed.

Now if he should be required to contend with those perpetual prisoners in "evaluating" these shadows while his vision was still dim and before his eyes were accustomed to the dark—and this time required for habituation would not be very short—would he not provoke laughter, and would it not be said of him that he had returned from his journey aloft with his eyes ruined and that it was not worth while even to attempt the ascent? And if it were possible to lay hands on and to kill the man who tried to release them and lead them up, would they not kill him?

They certainly would, he said.

(Trans. Paul Shorey; from *The Collected Dialogues of Plato*, eds. Edith Hamilton and Huntington Cairns [Princeton: Princeton University Press, 1969] 747–49)

This profound myth of Plato offers first the commanding metaphor of this investigation: the journey. As in the story the prisoner is freed from his shackles and allowed to move his head, and then turns around, sees the fire illuminating the cave, and consequently is marched up the ascent and through the entrance of the cave into the light of the sun, so is the present book an invitation to the reader to make a journey from darkness into light.

This metaphor of coming into the light is a deeply human one, what Carl Jung would probably call an archetype, and it can be seen to dominate three great axial or turning points in history.

The first is the Greek breakthrough from myth to logos, from common sense to scientific procedures. Paradoxically, in this myth Socrates (and Plato) are using a myth to signal the end of the age of myth. New techniques are coming into being, new ways of controlling reasoning, as Socrates laboriously teaches the Athenians the meaning of definition. This ability to define a word precisely, to say in other words its exact meaning and compass, will in turn give birth to logical inference and the syllogism. Already aborning in the Platonic dialogues, these laws of logic will be codified exhaustively by Aristotle. This in turn will give rise to a whole new ideal of science: the study of the universal and necessary through its causes. But the point here is that all this is evoked by Socrates in the image of a journey from darkness into light: a light which first dazzles and bewilders, but then is seen to be vastly preferable to the shadows which it replaces.

When Christianity begins, the dividing point of history on which our calendars still turn, the selfsame metaphor is evoked. As John prefaces the story of the Redeemer, "The real light which gives light to every man was coming into the world" (John 1:9). Later, he has Jesus himself saying, "I am the light of the world. No follower of mine shall ever walk in darkness; no, he shall possess the light of life" (John 8:12). Jesus' followers pick up the same image; in fact, it becomes the expression of their salvation, and the binding basis of their morality. "There was a time when you were darkness, but now you are light in the Lord. Well, then, live as children of light. Light produces every kind of goodness and justice and truth" (Eph 5:8-10). Those baptized, in later years, were often known technically as "the enlightened ones."

When the modern world came into existence, it appealed to the identical symbol. The En-lightenment, as the philosophical and cultural movement of the seventeenth and eighteenth centuries was called in English, represented the abandonment of the "dark ages," and the movement into the light of the modern world, illuminated now by science and the myth of progress. In Germany it was called *Aufklaerung*, in exact translation, the "Clearing Up," and in French *les Lumieres*, literally, the "Lights." In Italy it was known as *Illuminismo*, the "Illumination."

In this historical procession of images, then, from darkness to light—in the Greek breakthrough to science, in the Christian revelation of the inaccessible Light come into the world, in the modern move from the darkness of superstition into the light of science and technology—the present endeavor—with all due humility—would enroll itself. In its more modest way it, too, proposes a journey from darkness into the light of self-knowledge.

2

The Journey Proposed

Like "light and darkness," the "journey" is an archetypal reality, and some of its many aspects may be developed here.

A Personal Journey

As Socrates tells the story, it is a single individual that is selected to make the journey, the ascent, from darkness to light. His fellows remain in their places in the cave; they do not share in the experience of moving from darkness and immobility to light— at first blinding—and freedom. Even when this individual returns to the cave to share with the other prisoners his new-found illumination, he is initially confused by the darkness in which they live, and earns only their laughter.

Similarly, the journey the reader is invited to is a profoundly personal one.

In some journeys, one person can be substituted for by another. If a foreign head of state dies, the president of the United States may delegate his vice president to represent him at the funeral. A mother whose niece is marrying in a distant city may be able to send her daughter in her place. But other journeys simply cannot be undertaken by someone else. For example, no one could send a substitute on a honeymoon trip!

Again, a journey which has as its goal a personal experience can hardly be taken by another person. If someone is an excellent observer and writer, another may experience something vicariously through a travelogue. But, obviously, that is a pale substitute for the experience itself of a distant place. "Wish you were here" is a stock phrase for postcards sent home. Perhaps it means something like, "I wish you were here, so that you could be having the same rich experience I have, and sharing it with me; because there is no way a few words, even with a picture, can convey it to you."

Those journeys which mark a turning point in a human life share particularly this quality of personal agency. A momentous early journey is through the birth canal—it would be ludicrous to suggest one person could take that for another! As one matures, coming to self-consciousness and the age of reason, to the teenage quest for independence, to attaining the age of majority, at each stage, on a deeper level, one must make choices about who one will become that no one else can make. Indeed, if a parent tries to make those choices vicariously for a child, the personality of the child will be inhibited or even deeply stunted.

When two young people are attracted to each other, and begin to grow into a deeper relationship of friendship, they enter into a process in which no other can take their place. In literature, it is true, there are stories of one man trying to "pitch woo" for another—as with Captain John Smith and John Alden—but the woman, perhaps with a feminine intuition, discerns the true source, and scorns the substitute.

No matter how close their relationships, how many their friendships, individuals ultimately face their death alone. The journey into the netherworld no one can make for them.

The journey being proposed here is just such a personal journey. It is a journey that every person must make for himself or herself; no delegation to another is possible or even conceivable.

A Journey Within

Not only is the journey altogether personal; a further characteristic is that it is not an exterior journey, but a journey "within." That is placed in quotation marks, because it is obviously a metaphor.

In the Renaissance, thinkers distinguished between the macrocosm and the microcosm. The macrocosm was the larger world of their environment, just opening up with telescopes to almost unimaginable distances. But the microcosm was the human being—implying that here was another whole world to explore! It is that exploration of a personal and inner world which is intended here.

What is peculiar to an inner journey is that one seeks out activities rather than places. What is going on within myself? What regular activities take place there? These will be the guideposts for the inner journey.

An Arduous Journey

It would be dishonest to the reader to suggest that the journey in question will always be a pleasant, smooth, and easy one. The world within is at once familiar, and yet strangely foreign; the task of penetrating it, habituating oneself to and then systematically mapping its activities, requires prolonged attention, a sometimes frustrating and painful effort to understand, and an extended work of sifting perspectives and evidence before coming to a final and settled conclusion. One cannot help but think of a parallel in Jesus' words: "Enter through the narrow gate. The gate that leads to damnation is wide, the road is clear, and many choose to travel it. But how narrow is the gate that leads to life, how rough the road, and how few there are who find it!" (Matt 7:13).

In the story of the cave, the person does not simply rise up cheerily one day, cast off his chains, and stride gaily into the light. Rather, he is freed from his fetters, and "compelled to stand up suddenly and turn his head around and walk and to lift up his eyes to the light." In doing so, he experiences pain, and is so dazzled by the light that he can no longer discern even the shadows to which he was habituated before. Further, the ascent is "rough and steep," and someone must "drag him thence by force." One has the impression that the prisoner is hauled, kicking and screaming, into the light.

Those who are unwilling to expend a personal effort, to engage in a search for the light that will probably involve byways and dead ends, would probably do better to forget this project, and resign themselves to being simply prisoners in the cave.

A Momentous Journey

A choice about this journey can be profoundly consequential, because it may lead to a deeper knowledge of the self, which in turn may influence one's whole vision of reality. *Gnothe seauton*, "know thyself," was the inscription over the cave of the Delphic oracle. The injunction retains a deep wisdom. In sum, the personal journey within is a journey toward self-knowledge.

What precisely will be the fruit of this journey? Readers will want to know; then they could assess whether it would be worth the effort. Unfortunately, there is no way to summarize it in a few words. If it could be succinctly stated, it would remain meaningless, for the worth of the journey lies precisely in the experiences involved; without that experience, any formulae must perforce be abstract. But if I may give a personal testimony, to struggle to grapple with Lonergan's program of self-knowing and self-realization has profoundly changed my own mentality, so much so that I literally would find it all but impossible to reconstruct how I viewed reality before.

A Guide for the Journey

The theme of journey, as already suggested, is widespread in literature; in many cases the traveler also has a guide to strange and unknown places. In the myth of the cave, the agent of enlightenment is not so much as named, though his leading is obviously crucial; but one suspects that Plato may have had in mind Socrates himself. That suspicion is deepened when the story ends with the would-be enlightener of the other prisoners being put to death!

In the Book of Tobias, the angel Raphael ("God heals") guides the young Tobias, and sees him through many difficult passages, eventually bringing him home along with his lovely new-found bride and a medicine for his father's blindness.

In the *Divine Comedy* it is Virgil who is Dante's original guide through Hell and Purgatory. Many times Dante would have shrunk back in despair, and given up because of the obstacles; but Virgil always proves equal to the occasion.

The present author and the present book, then, offer themselves as guide for the journey. The need of a guide into one's very self may appear superfluous, but, as already intimated, and as hinted at by Plato's myth, the world within is familiar and yet altogether strange.

If the metaphor of Virgil's guidance may be pursued, however, he was not able to lead Dante into Paradise itself, since he was but a pagan. Eventually Dante needed another guide: Beatrice. The present author will be gratified if in due course the reader finds Lonergan himself to be an apt guide to higher places.

3

A Note on Metaphor

The notion of metaphor has been appealed to repeatedly in the preceding pages, and deserves an explicit comment. What is metaphor? It is a literary figure—an image or a set of words—which has a literal meaning, but also evokes another and figurative meaning. It is essential to keep the two meanings separate; the metaphor points to the figurative meaning, and it is a grave misunderstanding to confuse it with the literal meaning.

The myth of the cave, to begin, is a complex metaphor. One would misapprehend its thrust to think Socrates was speaking of a real cave somewhere; that one would hire a spelunker to explore the cave and determine that the ascent was, say, ninety feet long. The account itself suggests that it is a different and foreign meaning that Socrates would conjure up, as Glaucon observes, "A strange image you speak of, and strange prisoners."

Similarly, the idea of "journey" is used metaphorically. Journey has a literal meaning, and it has some bearing on the usage here; yet the journey intended is not a literal, but a figurative one. Again, the reader would be altogether mistaken if he began checking out airline flights or train schedules.

As already mentioned, the "within" that the journey seeks is also a metaphor. "Without" and "within" have very literal meanings: one can speak of the outside or inside of a box. The "within" indicated here is a different kind of thing, although it is not easy to say, especially at this stage of the journey, precisely what it does mean.

Darkness and light are also metaphors, used, as already seen, by Plato, early Christianity, and the Enlightenment to signify a movement from one state of humanity to another.

What is necessary to grasp a metaphor, then, is a certain nimbleness of mind—and here is another metaphor. Everyone is familiar with the nursery rhyme:

Jack be nimble,
Jack be quick;
Jack jump over the candlestick!

It describes a physical nimbleness. So what is a "nimbleness of mind"? It is like a physical nimbleness, and yet different. As a person must be physically nimble to jump over a candlestick, so one must be mentally nimble to grasp a metaphorical meaning, and not fall flat-footed onto the merely literal.

"Almost everything we say is a metaphor," Quintilian observed. That may in general be an exaggeration, but it is certainly true when it comes to the activities that the journey within is seeking to discover and catalogue; the rest of this chapter will explore some of these metaphors.

The central activity in the inner world of knowing, according to Lonergan, is "insight." The journey in prospect will only reveal and underline its centrality; but for now it is sufficient to note that a metaphor to physical sight, the sense of sight, is being invoked here. "Insight" is literally in-sight, looking into. This is a popular metaphor; how often we say, "Yes, I see," when we mean, "I see mentally." Children, perhaps unwittingly, underline the metaphorical versus the physical meaning when they repeat, "I see, said the blind man." The paradox is not unknown in literature; one thinks of the blind seer Teresias in *Oedipus Rex*. One senses that it is precisely because he cannot see physically that he enjoys the gift of prophetic vision.

"Intuition" is another word referring to mental activity which rests on the same metaphor, for the Latin *in-tuere* means to look into. "Introspection" has the very same structure.

The metaphor is extended also into "searching and finding." As he ran naked from the baths of Syracuse with his new-found insight into specific gravity, Archimedes cried, "Eureka" ("I have found it") from the Greek verb *heurisko*. Traces of the metaphor remain in the English word *heuristic*, to which attention will later return.

Knowing seems peculiarly associated with the sense of sight; hearing is typically associated with decision and choice. "I want you to do that right now—you hear!" we will say. The Latin word for "obey" is *obaudire*, literally to "hear against or in confrontation with."

Of the other senses, smell is rarely appealed to metaphorically, though an overly curious woman may be described as "nosy," and a person may say, "I smell a rat." Taste is occasionally used, when there is question of a profound knowledge which savors its object. "Taste and see how good the Lord is," one of the psalms has it.

Touch is sometimes appealed to—"Yes, you've put your finger on it!"—but more important is the associated image of holding, grasping with the hand, or the consequent possession. "Do you grasp what I'm saying," we will ask. "Yes, now I've caught on," may be the answer. More economically, "Do you get it?" "Yes, I have it now!" Another example is the German *Begriff*, which means "concept"; the original root is *greifen*, "to grasp." In Italian one says *capisco*—cognate with the Sicilian-American *capish*—"I take (it)."

The root "tend," meaning to tense, to stretch, to stretch toward, to reach for, can also be used for intellectual grasp. One might make an analogy: as searching is to seeing, so reaching is to grasping. The image can be found in the French *entendre*, "to understand," and the similar Spanish *entiendo*. In English the root applies more to choosing ("I intend to do that"), but it can have an intellectual reference as well, as in at-tend.

The posture of standing is also frequently appealed to. "I understand": literally, I stand under. This is a metaphor so long turned into a literal meaning that it is hard to capture the original reference. Does it perhaps suggest that when one stands under something, one grasps its intimate nature? A cognate word, however, is found in the German *verstehen*, "to understand." *Stehen*, of course, means "to stand"; the prefix *ver* usually means "thoroughly" or "completely"—perhaps to stand solidly, with a firm grasp of the issue.

In this plethora of images and languages, the reader may have lost the point (notice, a negative metaphor of seeking). The points are in fact two: the first is that the inner activities of knowing are so recondite and removed that one almost inevitably evokes them by appeal to sense and physical metaphors. The second point is that such metaphors must not be taken literally; they are meant to evoke, suggest, call up figuratively activities that are quite different from external, physical activities, or even from the operations of the senses. "Does that make sense?" one is tempted to quip.

Hoping the reader has seen these points, I suggest some homework: Why are "points" associated with understanding? What kind of metaphor is involved when we say that someone is intellectually "sharp"? or "dull"? This exercise may serve as a reminder this is a personal journey; the goal is not so much to memorize what someone else has indicated as intellectual metaphors, but to note for oneself the many metaphors one has used since learning the language, but probably without every having reflected on them very much.

4

Insight in Common Parlance

The myth of the cave evokes a journey within, and the entry point of that journey, as already suggested, will be found in the central act that Lonergan calls "insight." As already intimated, inner activities are at once familiar and strange; so, before venturing into one's own mind for a more exact observation of insight, it may be worth noting that it is an act of which common-sense people are quite aware, and which is already well attested to by ordinary language.

"Men—they just don't get it!" was the verdict of many women after watching the Anita Hill hearings in the confirmation of Supreme Court Justice Clarence Thomas. Apparently women grasped the "it" immediately, but to men it remained a mystery. Since the reader's guide happens to be a male of the species, it may also be beyond his ken. Fortunately, that is not important, because the present interest is in the "getting." What does it mean to "get" something? *That* both women and men understood; though women felt themselves to be "in the know," and men "in the dark," men also were quite well aware that the women were holding that an act of understanding, an insight, had failed to take place in them.

People of common sense may not be able to define "insight," but they are cognizant of the act and its implications. "See what I mean?" they will ask. "Do you catch my drift?" "Are you with me?" "Does that make sense to you?" "Do you catch on?" "Do you see what I'm driving at?" "Do you follow my meaning?" "Ya unnerstan'?" Do you get it yet?" These are all equivalent ways of asking the same question.

The positive response can be as varied. "Yeah, I follow you." "Go ahead—I've got the point." "Yes, I see exactly what you mean." "A word to the wise is sufficient." "I gotcha!" "You don't need to write me a book—I know what you mean already."

Sometimes insight is spoken of in a passive voice, as if it is something that happens to one, more than something one actively accomplishes. "It struck me that . . ."; "It dawned on me finally . . ."; "What occurred to me was . . ."; "The idea hit me between the eyes"; "It came to me like a thunderbolt."

The suddenness of the act is also often underlined. "Suddenly I realized . . ."; "All of a sudden it hit me . . ."; "Like a bolt out of the blue, I saw the solution."

Common parlance also brings out the fact that insight can be a matter of bringing disparate materials together. "All of a sudden, I saw the connection, which was never clear to me before." "How did I get it? I just put two and two together." "He has a wonderful ability to see connections that other people don't notice." Again, insight is often grasping a pattern that organizes materials until then disparate. "I was all at sixes and sevens, but she helped me to put it all together in my mind."

To this point the examples have focused on a positive understanding; but there is also the failure to understand, and ordinary language is quite capable of expressing that. "He just doesn't get it," as in the opening example. "She never catches a joke!" "I explained it to him very clearly, but it made absolutely no impression." "It never dawned on him to read the instructions." "The students will never catch on!" "She studied the material all night, but it still made no sense to her." "He memorized the procedure, but he never understood why it worked." "I explained it to her as best I could, but I drew a blank." "This is very difficult material—I'd estimate only one student in ten will get it."

In Mark's Gospel Jesus complains to his disciples. "Do you still not see or comprehend? Are your minds completely blinded? Have you eyes but no sight? Ears but no hearing? . . . Do you still not understand?" (8:17-18, 21).

A person who catches on quickly is called "insightful." That is also no foreign idea to common sense, which has many ways of expressing it. "He's bright, sharp, with it, catches on quickly, grasps what you mean before you finish explaining, never has to hear it twice. . . ." Common sense may also say, "The man's a genius, another Einstein, he should belong to Mensa, what an IQ!" Again, "She's brilliant, has a dazzling intelligence, never misses the point."

Common sense has an equally impressive array of words—often colorful—to disparage those who are slow to understand. "You're dumb, stupid, slow, dull." "You never catch on; you're a cretin, an idiot, an ignoramus." "He wasn't there the day they gave out the brains, there's nothing between his ears; the lights are on, but nobody's home." "She's a dumb-cluck, a half-wit, a dim bulb, she's a dumb-blond type." "He's your typical dumb brute, he's got a pea-brain, he's not bright enough to come in from the rain."

Common sense also recognizes various specializations of intelligence. It has ways of speaking of people with a technical or specialized intelligence, but who may lack common sense. The terms can express a range of attitudes from amused awe to deep contempt. "Nerd," "wonk," "dweeb," "a brain." "A pointy-headed bureaucrat who can't even park his bicycle straight." "An ivory-tower scientist"; "a mathematical genius, but without a lick of common sense." There's "the mad scientist," who "always has his head in the clouds," and "the absent-minded professor."

Insight can also be faked, and common-sense awareness is also wise to that possibility. "She's laughing at the joke, but I don't think she really got it." "He quotes everyone you can think of, but I'm not really convinced he knows what he's talking about." "C'mon, you know you don't have the slightest idea how to do it!" "You're just bluffing, we both know this goes completely over your head."

The point in the foregoing has not been to give a definition of insight—common sense rarely bothers its head about such precise statement. But it is to show that a common-sense grasp of insight is an implicit part of everyone's common-sense patrimony. None of the quotations above are in any way unusual—they could be heard in the home, the work place, the bar. Yet they point to the act Lonergan singles out as insight, they distinguish it from a lack of insight, they characterize people who have a ready understanding, as well as those who are slow to catch on; and they even reveal a sensitivity to different kinds of intelligence, the difference between a common-sense and a specialized understanding.

The reader is now in a position to ask, "Do I use these kinds of phrases? Have I ever paid attention to them before? What precisely do they mean?"

5

Insight in Sports

The time has come to turn from what common sense knows of insights to give some examples, and engage in a closer analysis of them. But the reader may be warned that the examples will not be earth shaking. They are not the insights that change the course of a person's life, much less a civilization's. In later chapters some of these will be examined, but the initial examples may appear so banal that the reader will wonder what the fuss is about. This is done for two reasons: (1) because most insights are in fact so ordinary that they go all but unnoticed, and (2) so that the reader will not be intimidated into thinking that insights are the aspirations only of great scientists or profound philosophers.

The initial example requires some background. As a boy, I loved to read the comics on Sunday morning. I grew up in the South, and so, during the winter, saw illustrated a world that was foreign to me: ice forts and sledding and throwing snowballs—or Snoopy ice-skating, his scarf flying behind him.

Recently I have been living in Boston, and often walk along the Charles River. It has frozen over, and one morning I noticed preparations for ice-skating: the snow had been cleared in a large oval, and there were hockey goals on the ice; smoke was rising from a small clubhouse. I had brought ice-skates for just such an occasion, and decided I would walk over in the afternoon.

Sure enough, when I arrived, young people were playing hockey on one end of the oval, and children and adults were skating on the other end. I had skated in rinks before, but now I realized I had a chance to achieve a childhood fantasy—skating out in the open, for free!

I wasn't sure if the clubhouse was private, so I sat down on a bench and put on my skates. I noted there was a wooden walk coming down from the clubhouse, with small pieces of wood across it serving as steps. But I was only a few paces from the ice, and strode confidently down the sloping bank.

Ka-boom! Suddenly I was sitting on my rear end, with both wrists smarting from breaking my fall. Two young girls asked solicitously if I was all right, and I assured them that I was, hoping to myself that my wrists were neither broken nor sprained. But I saw immediately what my mistake was: I had aligned the skates parallel to the slope—just like the young people coming down the wooden ramp—when I should have kept them perpendicular to the slope. When I did so, I was able to balance successfully, and side-step down to the ice.

When I thought about it a little, I realized I was facing a new situation here: at the rinks, there were always rubber mats between the area where skates were put on and the ice, and the mats were always level. As I thought about it more, however, I realized that the lesson was one I had already learned in skiing. An avid skier, I had never taken any lessons, but was self-taught; being an analytical person, however, I had given a fair amount of attention to the physics of the whole sport.

A ski slope is essentially an inclined plane. A beginner's slope has a gentle inclination. An intermediate slope has more of an angle, and an expert slope may be quite steep.

Beginner   Intermediate   Expert

When one first begins to ski, one learns the snow plow. This is accomplished by placing the skis in a wedge shape, and pushing the inner edges of the skis against the snow. What this does essentially is create friction, which means one will descend the slope more slowly. But speed increases with the square of the time, one might recall from physics, so that one is likely to accelerate down the slope. When one feels one is going too fast, or one's legs tire of holding the ski edges against the snow, then one has an emergency brake: sitting down, or falling down. That dramatically increases the friction, though one might find oneself still sliding quite a way to a stop.

As can be imagined, these first contrivances are rather unsatisfactory, not to mention inelegant. It didn't take me long to figure out that the secret was to ski sideways along the slope of the hill. The result of this was to take a single, steep incline, and turn it into a series of lesser inclines:

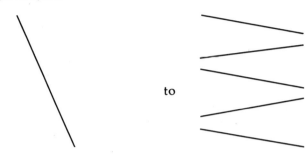

to

Stopping by this system is also simple: one just skies so that the incline becomes zero; or one even skies slightly up the slope, to break one's momentum.

That still leaves the turn because, at the edge of the slope—if one is not to go into the woods—one has to reverse direction and ski back across the other way. Inevitably that involves a moment when one is facing directly down the slope which, in the initial stages, can be terrifying. But rather than explaining the mysteries of snow-plow turns and the stem Christie, let us return to the original insight.

What was necessary to grasp was the relevance of the experience of stopping on a ski slope to that of maintaining one's balance on the river bank. This simple example illustrates a number of aspects of insight.

First, insight can take place very quickly, when the appropriate conditions are present. I had figured out the solution by the time I stood up.

Second, insight collates, it puts together, it connects. In this case, it connected what was learned on the ski slopes to a similar problem of keeping one's balance and controlling one's movement on an inclined plane, while wearing slippery runners.

Third, insight often involves memory. In this case, what had to be put together was a past learning and a present quandary. That is why a good memory is an important part of being intelligent. Remembering is not the same as understanding—there are those who remember everything and understand nothing—but it is often crucial to supplying the materials for an insight; a person of good memory and wide experience has a larger set of insights to apply to a new situation.

Fourth, insight grasps a pattern. A ski is much larger than a skate, and a skate blade much narrower than a ski. The sloped river bank hardly bore comparison to an awesome ski slope; yet the insight grasped that, in essence, the two situations were the same, and that the solution sufficing for one would work for the other.

Fifth, insight often takes place, as here, in a "cut-and-try" fashion. One is reminded—rudely and abruptly, in this case—that present procedures are not satisfactory, and one casts about for alternatives.

Sixth, insight is cumulative. It was because of insights on the ski slope that the skating problem was solved quickly and efficiently. In general, similar problems can be similarly understood, and have similar solutions.

Seventh, once an insight occurs, it is usually a permanent acquisition. Once a point is learned, it becomes easier to grasp it again in a similar circumstance.

Eighth, what is true for an individual is also true for the race. Euclid no doubt spent years working out all the proofs in his geometry, but any fairly intelligent high-schooler can learn them all in a semester.

Ninth, there is a disproportion between the "before" and the "after" of an insight. Before the insight occurs, no pattern is discerned, the materials jostle one another without being connected; one scratches one's head in complete puzzlement. But, once the insight has occurred, it may seem the simplest thing in the world; one only wonders why it took so long to catch on.

Tenth, this has implications for teaching, because teaching is essentially the mediation of insights. The teacher, who already has the insight, can point out the pattern to be recognized, emphasize what is similar, and play down what is irrelevant. The teacher cannot, however, have the insight for the student; that remains a personal acquisition.

Finally, one may ask what are the "appropriate conditions," mentioned above, for the insight to take place easily. They can be gathered from the foregoing: a good memory, a rich accumulation of past insights, a moderate to high degree of intelligence, a willingness to experiment, the past occurrence of a similar insight, or a good teacher. Similarly, by denying one or more of these conditions, one sees why insights can be sought laboriously, sometimes for years: a poor memory, little past experience, the lack of anyone else who understands the matter, and a situation or a problem that is quite different than any which have occurred previously—a question that demands breaking entirely new intellectual ground.

To this point, one simple insight has been in question, but it may also be noted that insights rarely occur singly; they cohere with past insights, and they suggest new lines of inquiry. So the insight into inclined planes on the ski slope required an examination of turning procedures. But the inclined planes might just as well have brought to mind Galileo's experiments of rolling balls of different weights down inclined planes. Undoubtedly there would be connections between his discoveries and the physics of the ski slope. For example: does a small child or a heavier adult go faster on skis? Further, as Galileo came to an equation between distance and time for a falling body, so one might want a formula for the speed of a skier, which would have to include the steepness of the slope, the angle of incline of the skier's path, the length of the skis, the amount and kind of wax on the skis, the consistency of the snow, and so on.

The insight above might have led off in other directions. For example, anyone who has done mountain driving with its hair-pin turns has seen the same idea of many inclined planes illustrated in another way. Also, basic insights often require more refined insights to complement them: as I experimented more that afternoon with negotiating the river bank, I discovered that a very small angle of departure from the perpendicular could be potentially destabilizing.

This chapter may have seemed to the reader at once too simple and too complicated. The initial insight may have appeared to be too trivial to be worth mention, and all the implications drawn from it far too complex. But the list is neither exhaustive nor even normative; its intention rather is to function as an invitation to readers to note their own insights, to see what they put together, under what conditions they occur or do not occur and, perhaps, what patterns obtain between them.

6

Insight and the Detective Story

A detective story is usually the story of a murder—a drama of death, violence, and the hatred or greed that occasioned the act. But, in another way, it may be thought of as the search for an insight, or set of insights, that explains the initial mystery. The "whodunit," it is often called, thus setting the question that lends interest to the story. At times the murder may take place "offstage": it is merely the setting. The allure of the story is in figuring out what happened, and usually the reader matches wits with the detective.

The reader is furnished with a set of clues. Of course, they are not necessarily labelled as such, and the reader must first be alert enough to recognize their significance. Also, there may be false clues, which point in the wrong direction, and dead-end clues, which lead nowhere. Out of this welter of detail the reader and the detective are left to make some sense. Usually the detective has, at some point, his suspicions; at some juncture, it all falls into place for him. The reader, unless he or she is very intelligent, normally lags behind, and sees the pattern and grasps the identity of the murderer only after the final explanation is given. But all the clues were there and, in the best kind of detective story, the reader can go back and say, "Why didn't I see it?"

Probably the best-known detective, to English-language readers, is Arthur Conan Doyle's Sherlock Holmes. (See *The Complete Sherlock Holmes* [Garden City, N.Y.: Doubleday, 1930].) His abilities of observation and deduction have become legendary, and have passed into common parlance.

As portrayed by his friend Watson, Holmes describes himself in the first mystery, *A Study in Scarlet*, as a man who "has a turn both for observation and deduction" (23). To that he adds a vast set of background insights, his knowledge of the history of crime. Since criminality has a certain repetitiveness, his background knowledge suggests to him helpful parallels. He is adamant that his system is not mere guesswork, but a "Science of Deduction" (19), whose conclusions are "as infallible as propositions of Euclid" (23), to use Watson's expression.

In *The Sign of Four* Holmes expands on the difference between observation and deduction. He states that Watson went to the Post Office to send a telegram; Watson wants to know how he figured that out. Part was observation: a red mud was caked on Watson's shoe, which could only have come from the place in the street where, in front of the Post Office, work was going on. But the rest was deduction—Watson had written no letter, he had plenty of stamps—and so the only reason he might have gone to the Post Office would have been to post a telegram. Insight is in play here in either case, because it makes the connection between the mud on Watson's boot and the memory of the street work being done; but it also grasps the possibilities for which Watson might have gone to the Post Office.

More astounding are the inferences made from Watson's watch. To test Holmes, Watson gives him a watch, and asks him what it says about its former owner. Holmes concludes that the watch descended from Watson's father, through his elder brother, to him. He further describes the older brother as "a man of untidy habit—very untidy and careless. He was left with good prospects, but he threw away his chances, lived for some time in poverty with occasional short intervals of prosperity, and, finally, taking to drink, he died" (92).

This is so close to the mark that Watson accuses Holmes of having secretly investigated his brother. But Holmes explains it all from the watch. The father and the elder brother he gets from the initials, and the fact that jewelry is often passed down to the eldest son. The carelessness of the brother is established by the dents all over the watch case, meaning he had kept the watch in his pocket with coins or keys. From the quality of the watch he gleans the brother's original affluence. From marks on the inside of the case he knows the watch has been with the pawnbrokers numerous times, showing both the poverty and the occasional moments of prosperity (without which he could not have reclaimed the watch). The keyhole, finally, for winding the watch, has tiny scratches all around it— the sign of a drunkard fumbling at the nightly winding.

"Where is the mystery in all this?" (93) Holmes challenges. "It is as clear as daylight" (93), concedes Watson. And it is not hard to see here the work of insight, which grasps the connection between the initials and the father, between the dents and the keys and the carelessness, between the price of the watch and the brother's initial prosperity, between the marks of the pawnbrokers and the brother's financial ups and downs, between the scratches around the keyhole and the owner's habitual drinking.

Holmes, as Watson pictures him, is a man who literally lives to think. Indeed, if he has no intellectual stimulus, he becomes so deathly bored as to take cocaine. "I cannot live without brainwork. What else is there to live for?" (93). This lends Holmes a certain detached, uninvolved air. He chides Watson for romanticizing him in *A Study in Scarlet.* "Detection is, or ought to be, an exact science and should be treated in the same cold and unemotional manner. You have attempted to tinge it with romanticism, which produces much the same effect as if you worked a love story or an elopement into the fifth proposition of Euclid" (90).

Almost immediately the story goes on to an event that underlines this: a young woman comes to present to Holmes a perplexing problem. As she leaves, Watson muses, "What a very attractive woman!" (96). Holmes responds languidly, "Is she? I did not notice." Faced with this contradiction to Holmes's usual keen powers of observation, Watson cries, "You really are an automaton—a calculating machine. There is something positively inhuman in you at times" (96).

Of all the Conan Doyle stories, perhaps the best known is *The Hound of the Baskervilles.* A particularly eerie background sets the tone: the geographical placement of the Baskerville baronial house on the moor, and the legendary story of Hugo Baskerville, a rogue who died on the moor, his throat ripped out by a supernatural hound from hell. Sir Charles Baskerville has just died at the house under mysterious circumstances, apparently frightened to death; and his nephew, Henry Baskerville, the last of the line, has come to take over the house. Newly arrived in London from America, he seeks out Sherlock Holmes's help.

As the story begins, Holmes once again gives a casual demonstration of his deductive powers. A Dr. Mortimor has visited, a friend of Henry Baskerville, and forgotten his walking stick in Holmes's rooms. From a close examination of the stick, and the enigmatic inscription upon it, "To James Mortimor, M.R.C.S., from his friends of the C.C.H., 1884" (667), Holmes deduces that it belongs to a country doctor, who had once practiced in the city; that he had been a senior student in London, at the Charing Cross Hospital, and now was "a young fellow under thirty, amiable, unambitious, absent-minded, and the possessor of a favourite dog, which I should describe roughly as being larger than a terrier and smaller than a mastiff" (671).

How does Holmes arrive at these conclusions? He explains: "It is my experience that it is only an amiable man in this world who receives testimonials, only an unambitious one who abandons a London career for the country, and only an absent-minded one who leaves his stick and not his visiting-card after waiting an hour in your room" (671). As for the dog, he has often carried the staff behind his master, and his teeth marks are too wide for a terrier, but not broad enough for a mastiff.

Again, the role of insight is clear, in connecting the inscription to the testimonial and the amiability, the shift to the country to the lack of ambition, the forgotten stick to the absent-mindedness, and the width of the canine teeth marks to the size of the dog. "Elementary, my dear Watson!"

The first clue to the mystery of the Baskervilles emerges when Henry Baskerville, just arrived in London, has a new boot stolen, then an old one. The events may seem trivial, disconnected; but Holmes saw immediately it was to put a hound on Henry's scent, which meant it was not a supernatural hound at all! The second clue is not made known to the reader until later: Holmes notes a faint smell of perfume on a warning note sent to Henry in London. That turns his suspicions on Stapleton, a naturalist, and his sister, neighbors of the Baskervilles on the moor. Already Holmes is moving toward an insight. "The thing takes shape, Watson. It becomes coherent" (685).

The note read as follows: "As you value your life or your reason keep away from the moor" (685). All but the last word was clipped from a printed text and pasted on the page. Holmes recognizes the typeface immediately, calls for the previous day's *Times*, and reads out a passage: "You may be cajoled into imagining that your own special trade or your own industry will be encouraged by a protective tariff, but it stands to reason that such legislation must in the long run keep away wealth from the country, diminish the value of our imports, and lower the general conditions of life in this island" (686).

Holmes has obviously had an insight, as he rubs his hands in high glee. But his companions have not. Sir Henry confesses, "I don't know much about the tariff and things like that kind, but it seems to me we've got a bit off the trail so far as that note is concerned" (686). Even Watson, more familiar with Holmes's methods, is forced to say, "No, I confess that I see no connection" (686). But Holmes insists they are rather hot upon the trail.

Perhaps the reader may be in the same quandary as Holmes's companions; but some strategically placed italics may help: "*You* may be cajoled into imagining that *your* own special trade *or your* own industry will be encouraged by a protective tariff, but it stands to *reason* that such legislation must in the long run *keep away* wealth *from the* country, diminish the *value* of our imports, and lower the general conditions of *life* in this island" (686).

(The alert reader may note, however, that Conan Doyle made a slip: there is no "As" in the quotation. Further, he catches only two of the three "doublets" present, "keep away" and "from the," missing the "or your.")

Holmes confesses that the case is a highly puzzling one, suggesting an addition to the last chapter's list of reasons why insight might come slowly: the sheer difficulty of the matter. Holmes allows he does not comprehend as yet: "Well, I don't profess to understand it yet. This case of yours is very complex, Sir Henry. When taken in conjunction with your uncle's death I am not sure that of all the five hundred cases of capital importance which I have handled there is one which cuts so deep" (693). But Watson is able at least to formulate the direction of solution.

> Another item had been added to that constant and apparently purposeless series of small mysteries which had succeeded each other so rapidly. . . . Holmes sat in silence as we drove back to Baker Street, and I knew from his drawn brows and keen face that his mind, like my own, was busy in endeavoring to frame some scheme into which all these strange and apparently disconnected episodes could be fitted (696).

It would be hard to find a better characterization of insight!

Another clue comes when Watson meets Stapleton and his sister.

> There could not have been a greater contrast between brother and sister, for Stapleton was neutral tinted, with light hair and gray eyes, while she was darker than any brunette whom I have seen in England—slim, elegant, and tall. She had a proud, finely cut face, so regular that it might have seemed impassive were it not for the sensitive mouth and the beautiful dark, eager eyes. With her perfect figure and elegant dress she was, indeed, a strange apparition upon a lonely moorland path. . . . She spoke in a low, eager voice, with a curious lisp in her utterance (709).

In time it turns out that the Stapletons are not brother and sister at all, but man and wife; he met her in one of his former lives in South America.

Stapleton drops another clue when he mentions he worked at a school in northern England. Holmes is able to get educational records and a picture of a "Mr. and Mrs. Vondeleur" (753), obviously the Stapletons in another guise.

In the meantime the butler gives Watson another clue: a letter burned in the grate on the night of Sir Charles's death, with the initials "L.L." still visible as a signature. Watson is able to trace it to a Laura Lyons of a nearby village. He confronts her with the question of her relationship to Sir Charles, and the letter written the day of his death. When he reports the conversation to Sherlock Holmes, the latter expresses satisfaction: "It fills up a gap which I had been unable to bridge in this most complex affair" (742).

But it is when Holmes reveals to Watson that the Stapletons are really husband and wife that it all falls into place for Watson. "All my unspoken instincts, my vague suspicions, suddenly took shape and centered upon the naturalist" (742). (The suddenness of insight is nicely mirrored here.) This identification is confirmed when, a little later, Holmes visits Baskerville Hall for the first time. All through supper he stares at one of the Baskerville portraits—that of the original rogue, Hugo. After supper, when Sir Henry has gone to his room, and Holmes has Watson alone, he stands upon a chair and covers the hat and the long ringlets surrounding Hugo's face. "Good heavens," Watson cried in amazement. It was the face of Stapleton which had sprung out from the canvas! Holmes explains, "My eyes have been trained to examine faces and not their trimmings" (750). Insight grasps the true parallels between two situations or realities, and is able to ignore the more trivial differences.

Now all the pieces have fallen into place. "This chance of a picture," Holmes says, "has supplied us with one of our most obvious missing links" (750). Stapleton is really the unknown son of the ne'er-do-well brother of Sir Charles who had died in South America. With Charles and Henry out of the way, he would be the next in line to inherit the vast Baskerville fortune. Presently Holmes is able to say, "I shall soon be in the position of being able to put into a single connected narrative one of the most singular and sensational crimes of modern times" (753).

The interest here is not in the Baskervilles, or their supernatural hound, nor even in Holmes and Watson and their detective methods, but in the nature of insight. For the journey being undertaken is not an outer one, to London or the moor, but an inner one, into the functioning and activities of the mind. But there remains one concluding reflection upon insight that may be garnered from this murder mystery. In the last chapter it was noted that insight is very difficult before it occurs, but deceptively simple after it has taken place. Holmes makes a remarkably similar comment: "The whole course of events, from the point of view of the man who called himself Stapleton, was simple and direct, although to us, who had no means in the beginning of knowing the motives of his actions and could only learn part of the facts, it all appeared exceedingly complex" (761).

7

Insights in Jokes

"Getting a joke," "catching on to a joke" are common-sense phrases that suggest that jokes also involve insight. This may seem a less than serious field in which to pursue the investigation of mental activities; but, as will soon appear, the lowly joke actually involves a fairly sophisticated pattern of insights.

> The man sat at a piano bar. The piano player's pet cat was on the piano, and generally making a nuisance of himself. Finally, in exasperation, the man went to the piano player and said, "Do you know your cat's got his tail in my Margarita?" "No," the piano player answered. "But if you can hum a few bars of it, I'll try and pick up the melody."

The French word *entendre*, "to understand," has already been noted; used even in English is the phrase *double entendre*, a "double understanding or meaning." The second meaning is usually sexual, but this is not necessary; many jokes function on the principle of a double understanding. In the joke being considered here, the man at the bar understands one thing: he is lodging a complaint about a trying cat. The piano player has another understanding: he thinks the man is asking for a song. Note that, in the story, each understanding has its own plausibility: the man's reaction to the annoying cat is grounded in the tale, while the piano player's expectation is based on the generally known fact that such performers take requests. Note, further, that only the speaker and listener to the joke have the double understanding: the piano player does not understand the man's concern, and the man, at least as he approaches the piano player, does not think he will be understood as asking for a song. Even such a simple joke, then, which is normally caught almost immediately, has a fairly complex structure. It is actually three insights; getting the joke requires understanding at once the man's understanding, the piano player's understanding, and their mutual incomprehension. It may be diagrammed this way:

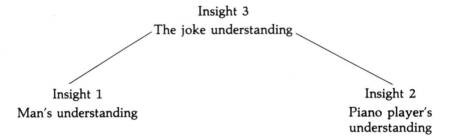

Further, if the reader has understood the point here, then he or she has a fourth insight, which grasps the above three insights in their proper interrelationships.

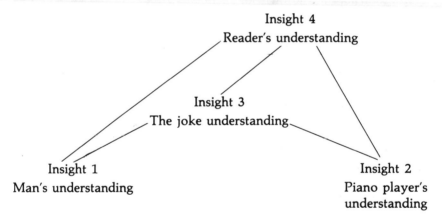

Insight, then, can bear on other insights, grasping the connection between them, understanding the pattern of their interrelationships. A crowning or key insight may even grasp a whole range of subordinate insights.

Jokes do not really bear so much analysis; usually they are either understood immediately, or are hardly worth explaining. But, as the aim here is not so much humor as understanding, such laborious examination of the mechanism of the joke may be forgiven.

> A woman suffering from a cold was going to a fancy dinner party.
> Knowing she would not have her purse at the table, she stuffed a

couple of extra handkerchiefs into her bra. During the meal she felt the need for a handkerchief, and searched discreetly on one side, and found nothing; then on the other side, and again found no handkerchief. More determinedly, she fished again on the one side, then on the other. Suddenly she realized that conversation had totally stopped around the table, and all eyes were fixed on her. Totally nonplussed, she blurted out, "But I'm sure I had two when I came!"

Again, there are two understandings. The woman in her statement is referring to the handkerchiefs. The dinner guests, of course, know nothing of the errant handkerchiefs, and so conclude that she must be speaking of her breasts. Only the listener grasps both understandings at once.

The foreigner was trying, with his limited English, to explain that his wife was infertile. "You see," he said, "my wife is impregnable." Catching the blank looks of his audience, the perplexed foreigner tried again. "What I mean," he said, "is that my wife is unbearable." Again perceiving their incomprehension, and the beginning of a smile on the faces of some of his listeners, the hapless man tried again. "That is, my wife is inconceivable!"

The pattern here is more complex. The foreigner has in mind the idea he is trying to communicate, but the words he is using convey a different meaning. "Impregnable" is a description that might apply to a fort, not to a woman. The listeners understand this, and grasp at the same time that this is not what the man intends; hence their blank stares. Again, "unbearable" would mean "insupportable, the kind of person one cannot put up with"; this is not only not what the man means, but is outrageous enough to cause a snicker. Finally, the man uses the word "inconceivable," which is usually used metaphorically, not for a physical, but for a mental conception. In each case, however, there is a certain plausibility to the foreigner's stab at communication: "pregnant" is not so far from "pregnable"; "bearing a child" is related to "unbearable"; and "inconceivable" is not altogether diverse from "unable to conceive." Effortlessly, in most cases, the joke-insight grasps all these insights and lack of insights, the "close but no cigar" nature of each of the approximations. Note that this joke uses another favorite method of humor: repetition. Essentially the same joke is repeated three times, exploiting the possibilities of the English language for a growing incongruity.

Incongruity is another element of humor, present in many jokes. The understanding of the dinner guests above was one example: they understood the woman to be saying she had lost one or both of her breasts, when everyone knows that one cannot lose a body part while sitting at a dinner table.

Children love to tell the elephant jokes. "How can you tell if an elephant has been in your refrigerator?" "By the footprints in the butter." Here there are not two people who carry the double insight, but the three-fold structure can still be traced. The listener grasps at once the size of a stick of butter, the size of an elephant's foot, and the total incongruity of the one with the other. More generally, the whole picture is riddled with incongruity: elephants are so large that they dwarf, not just sticks of butter, but even refrigerators; the original idea of the elephant in the refrigerator is nonsense.

Pursuing the analysis further, one might speak of a backward, or inverse, insight. Usually when one speaks of A being within B, it is assumed that A is smaller than B. In this case that normal expectation is upset, and one grasps that the expectation created by the phrase "an elephant in a refrigerator" involves an impossible juxtaposition. The incongruity of the elephant in the refrigerator, then, is only doubled in the idea of the footprint in the butter.

Many jokes function in this way: they create one set of expectations, only to dash them with an incongruous outcome.

> For some time the man had noted the ringing in his ears, and finally went to his doctor to have it checked. The doctor peered into his ears, did a number of tests, and conceded he didn't understand the problem; the patient would have to see a specialist, an ear doctor.
>
> The ear doctor also did his examination, and more extensive testing; but in the end he, too, confessed himself baffled, and suggested that the patient consult a brain specialist.
>
> The brain specialist did a CAT scan, and many other tests, but even he was unable to explain the ringing in the man's ears. "It could be something serious," he said; "frankly, I can't guarantee you more than six months to live."
>
> The man felt healthy, except for the ringing in his ears, so he decided he should enjoy fully what might be the last six months of his life. He quit his job, cashed in his stocks, and signed up for an around-the-world tour. Thinking he would need some new clothes for the fancy dinner parties aboard ship, he bought four new suits, expensive ones, and then went to the shirt counter.
>
> The salesman said, "I'd say you were a size 14 neck."
>
> "No," the man responded. "I'm a 13."
>
> The salesman measured and said, "It's just as I thought; you're a size 14."
>
> "That's not true!" the man insisted. "I've always worn a 13."
>
> "I'll give you a 13 if that's what you want," the salesman responded.
>
> "But I warn you—you're going to have a ringing in your ears!"

The incongruity here is that the man's problem was not discovered by any of the specialists, but is recognized immediately by the shirt salesman; and that the difficulty, which seemed so complex to the specialists, turned out to have such a simple explanation. One might note here a double failure of expectations: the insight is not where it would be expected, among the specialists, but is where it would not be expected, with the shirt salesman.

> A man had sought for years for the secret of life. He had read and meditated and prayed, and consulted priests and rabbis and psychologists and gurus without number; but their answers as to the secret of life left him always unsatisfied. Finally someone told him of a wise old man who lived high in the Himalayas. At great expense, both financial and personal, he traveled there, kept asking directions, and finally encountered the man at the door of his cave late one afternoon. He greeted him reverently, sat down ceremoniously, and posed his question, "O Master, what is the secret of life?"
>
> "Life," the seer answered portentously, "is a fountain."
>
> "Life is a fountain?" the man responded. "What do you mean, 'Life is a fountain'? Did I travel all this way just to have you tell me, 'Life is a fountain?' "
>
> "You mean it isn't?" the seer replied.

The incongruity here lies in the fact that one would assume that the seer's insight was one he had investigated and verified in a lifetime of experience, thought, and meditation; one would not expect it to be upset by a visitor's question. To put it another way, the insight of the seer would obviously have been one he had built his whole life on; it is incongruous to see that whole foundation crumble at the impatient question of the man sitting at his feet.

> The parents were worried about their boy; he was just impossibly optimistic, and they were concerned that he was not being sufficiently prepared for the disappointments of the real world. As Christmas approached, they made preparations for a last, desperate attempt to bring him down to earth, and moderate his expectations. On Christmas morning they led him to a room in the house; when he opened it, he found it stacked to the ceiling with horse manure!
>
> "Quick!" the boy shouted. "Get a shovel! With all this manure, there has to be a horse in there somewhere!"

Everything in the story suggests that the boy will be disappointed at Christmas; but the expectation is upset, and his optimism triumphs even over this intended disappointment.

Again, there are two understandings: the parents see a room full of horse manure as the most disappointing thing they could think of for Christmas. But the boy sees rather a symbol of possibility, the sign of the animal vitality necessary to produce all this waste.

What this suggests is that insight has a certain freedom in relation to the materials it understands. The parents and the boy "see" the same room and the same manure, physically; yet how differently they "see" it intellectually! Well known is the distinction between the pessimist and the optimist: to the pessimist, the glass is half empty; to the optimist, it is half full. It is, of course, the same glass.

> The foursome were playing golf when a funeral cortege passed by. One of the men doffed his hat and stood at silent and reverent attention until the hearse was out of sight.
>
> Awed, one of the foursome said to him, "I gather this person must have meant something special to you?"
>
> "Oh," the man explained, "I thought it the least I could do when the woman lived with me for 37 years."

Here one might notice a double reversal of expectations. The first is that, normally, a golfer would pay no attention to a passing funeral procession. But the deeper incongruity emerges when one realizes the person being buried is the man's wife. Here, the expectation is the opposite: that the man would be attending the funeral, and not playing golf! The person who gets the joke, then, grasps the social meaning of a golf game, the social demands of a funeral, and the fact that the one is incongruously placed before the other.

> The graduate student came into the psychology class and explained he was doing a survey to verify an hypothesis: that people's happiness is in direct proportion to the frequency with which they have sex. So he asked how many had sex at least once a day; a small number raised their hands, but all were beaming. Then he asked how many had sex twice a week; a larger number raised their hands; they too appeared happy, though not quite as enthusiastic. Those who identified themselves as having sex once a week appeared no more than satisfied; whereas the ones who claimed to have sex once a month looked positively glum. Finally, the investigator asked, "Is there anyone who has sex as little as once a year?" In the back of the room a hand shot up, the student waving wildly and enthusiastically. Shaken, the graduate student said, "That disqualifies my whole theory! How can you be so happy, when you have sex so infrequently?"
>
> "Tonight's the night!" the student exclaimed.

A double reversal can be noted here. The initial understanding is set by the investigator's hypothesis. The first four answers fit perfectly, but the last answer appears to conflict. When one grasps the student's answer, however, the original hypothesis is vindicated after all, and with a vengeance! The insight of the joke, then, grasps all these converging and conflicting understandings, and the way that a seeming conflict actually turns into a confirmation.

> The 70-year-old man was at the end of his yearly physical. The doctor said admiringly, "You're a remarkable physical specimen! You have the body of a 50-year-old. Would you mind my curiosity if I asked how old your father was when he died?"
>
> "Did I say my father died?" the man retorted.
>
> "Oh, I'm sorry," said the doctor. "Do you mean he's still living?"
>
> "He certainly is," said the man. "He's 92, and he plays golf every Tuesday if it's good weather!"
>
> "Remarkable!" the doctor responded. "Would you mind if I asked how old your grandfather was when he died?"
>
> "Did I say my grandfather died?" the man questioned.
>
> "You don't mean to say he's still living!" said the doctor. "How old is he?"
>
> "Exactly 111," the man said. "And not only that, but he's getting married next Saturday!"
>
> "Getting married!" the doctor marveled. "What would a 111-year-old man want to get married for?"
>
> "Did I say he *wanted* to get married?" the man demanded.

What may be noted here is that questions often bear presuppositions and understandings within them. "Have you stopped beating your wife?" is the proverbial example: it implies that one had been engaged in such an activity. Here the doctor's questions imply the death of both the father and the grandfather. Part of the humor is to see these expectations reversed in the patient's indignant response. This joke also exploits repetition, as "Did I say . . ." becomes almost a ritual response. The final insight is again into a double insight: the doctor's understanding of why an old man would *want* to get married, and the patient's implication that his grandfather *had* to get married—presumably because he had gotten a woman pregnant. The double incongruity, then, is not only that the grandfather of a 70-year-old man would still be alive, but that he would be potent enough to impregnate a woman.

As already mentioned, the point of this chapter is not so much to get readers to chuckle as to engage their curiosity about how humor "works." The next time the reader hears a joke, he or she should pause to reflect on the way it functions, and the insights, often multiple, that it involves.

8

Great Insights in Science

Most of the insights considered so far have been relatively trivial; but there are also insights that change lives, ground new industries, change the course of whole civilizations. Some of the most striking instances are found in the history of science, and this chapter will examine briefly four such instances to widen and render more precise the account of insight.

Galileo

Galileo Galilei was one of the bright lights of the beginnings of modern science. He was born in 1564 and died in 1642. Famous among his insights is one that took place in the cathedral of Pisa in 1581, while he was studying there as a young man. A sacristan drew a hanging lamp to himself, worked on it, and then released it. Like a pendulum, its motion described a series of arcs. Galileo noticed something no one else had: though the height of the swings decreased, the time for each complete cycle (the period) was the same.

Galileo had, of course, no wristwatch or stopwatch to time the swings; he measured them by his pulse. His insight, then, was to grasp a connection between the regularity of his pulse and the regularity of the swings. As with many scientific insights, it was a backward or inverse insight: the width of the swings—contrary to what one might naturally expect— was not significant for the time to traverse one cycle.

As it turned out, the only significant variable was the length of the pendulum. Neither the weight of the bob at the end, nor the height of the swings, was important to the time of the period of the pendulum.

This insight illustrates a number of things about scientific insight. The first is that observation is required. Until Galileo's time philosophers had often reasoned about things, about how they had to be. Galileo reflects the spirit of the new physical science when he sets out to discover how in fact they are.

Second, this determination is usually made by measurement. It was not enough to speculate on whether the period of the swings required the same amount of time, as the range of the swing decayed; one must measure it exactly—for which Galileo used the best measure he had at hand, his pulse. Clearly, one direction science will take will be more and more exact measurement.

Third, science wants an insight that sidelines as many extraneous factors as possible, to grasp a minimal number of significant elements. In this case, the height of the lamp above the floor, the age of the sacristan, the amount of push he may have imparted to the lamp, the color of the glass, the weight of the lamp, the range of the swing—all are abstracted from, to grasp the interrelation of just two factors: the length of the pendulum, and the time required to traverse one cycle. The length of the pendulum, also, becomes an idealized quantity: it is calculated from the point of the pivot to the center of gravity of the bob. The chain supporting it is considered, for purposes of calculation, to be an infinitely thin string.

One might think the obvious use of this insight would be to design time pieces. In fact, that was done later on, and the pendulum-driven grandfather clock is still in use. As any parent who has had a child on a swing knows, to keep a constant swing going requires a tiny push at the top of each swing. This is accomplished in the grandfather clock by the escapement mechanism, which, in turn, receives its energy from the slowly descending weight. But the immediate use Galileo put it to was medicine. Reversing the relation of pendulum to pulse, he invented a mechanism in which the length of the pendulum could be increased or diminished until it corresponded exactly with a patient's pulse. Then the length of the pendulum would tell the doctor if the pulse was fast or slow.

One refining insight before closing: in fact, more accurate measurement showed that the period of the pendulum was not precisely the same over wide variations in the swing. Historians debate whether Galileo was aware of this or not. In any case, the discrepancy was not large enough to be significant for the uses to which Galileo applied the insight.

Newton

Perhaps the best-known insight in all of science is that associated with Isaac Newton (1642–1727) under the apple tree. The plague is raging in London, and Newton returns from his university studies to his home at Woolsthorpe. He is only twenty-four. As he sits in the garden, an apple falls to the ground with a soft thud. Newton has an insight that is to dominate earthly and celestial mechanics for almost the next three centuries. What did he understand?

Sherlock Holmes distinguished observation and deduction, and there appears a similar division of labor in science. Kepler had already analyzed the movements of the planets, and shown that their speed was related to the square of their distance from the sun. The question was, *Why* was that the case? The work of the deductive scientist was necessary as Newton came on the scene. He had no laboratory equipment, no telescopes, only his intelligence, as he sat in the garden, under the apple tree.

To understand his insight, some background explanation of Newton's first law of motion is necessary. Imagine a parent, again, pushing a child in a wagon. The wagon keeps moving as long as the parent is pushing. As soon as the parent stops—unless the wagon is on an incline—the wagon also soon slows to a stop, and the child is likely to be crying, "Push me again!" The normal expectation, then, is that whatever is not pushed comes to rest.

Galileo had already established what Newton formulated in the first law of motion: whatever is moving will continue moving indefinitely, unless something stops it. That, of course, flatly contradicts what one might normally expect; it is another example of that backward, or inverse, kind of insight, which grasps that movement is no different from rest. Just as what is at rest stays so, unless a force acts upon it, so something in motion stays so, moving at exactly the same speed, and in the same direction, unless a force acts on it.

The difference between the parent's expectation and the first law of motion is, of course, friction. The wagon slows down because of the friction of the wheels on the pavement and of the bearings on the axles. Newton's first law of motion, however, sees the friction as merely an unimportant factor to be abstracted from. If there were no friction, the wagon would roll on forever. This is not entirely opposed even to common-sense expectations. If one oils the bearings, the wagon will roll further. An ice hockey puck given a vigorous shove will continue moving for a long distance, because the friction is minimal. One only has to idealize that thought: if the friction is reduced to zero, then the motion will continue forever, in a straight line, at exactly the same speed.

In the scientific mode, then, Newton's first law abstracts from friction as an irrelevant variable, and so focuses on speed and direction as to grasp that rest and motion are essentially the same; in one case the speed is zero, in the other it is some positive quantity, but in either case the state will endure until some outside force acts on the resting or moving body.

Now Newton was thinking about the moon. It was obviously moving. By his first law, then, it should remain in perpetual motion in a straight line, unless some force were acting on it. But it wasn't moving in a straight line, it was moving in a circle, in its orbit around the earth. So some force must be acting on it to divert it from straight-line motion. What could that force be?

Newton saw the apple fall to the ground. He knew the earth had attracted the apple: Galileo had already quantified the movement of a falling body. But what Newton saw was that the moon might be the same as the apple! As the earth draws the apple, so it was drawing the moon, diverting it from straight-line to circular motion.

Newton saw that distance would be one of the factors involved. The force of gravity, it stood to reason, would become weaker as it acted further and further from the earth, especially since that force would be dispersing in all directions from the earth. Kepler's compilations already suggested the inverse square law: that the force would diminish as the square of the distance.

The other element was mass. Since the moon was a great deal larger than the apple, it would be drawn more strongly to the earth; but since it was so much further away, it would be drawn more weakly than the apple. Newton's hypothesis was that the two would balance out—the near distance of the apple with its minor mass, and the far distance of the moon with its much larger mass—so that the apple and the moon would be drawn with the same force.

In trying to make the calculations, however, one is faced with a question: How far is the apple from the earth? That seems like a trivial question: "It depends on the height of the tree," one is tempted to answer. But it becomes more difficult when one reflects that the apple might be six feet from one part of the earth and some eight thousand miles from another part, on the opposite side of the globe! So which distance does one use? Here Newton utilizes another scientific idealization: the earth is considered, for purposes of computation, as a single point, at the center of gravity of the earth, with all its mass concentrated at that point. The distance of the apple from the earth, then, is the radius of the earth, plus the height of the tree, or, roughly, four thousand miles.

An historical anomaly illustrates the sometimes serendipitous nature of scientific insight. Though Newton made the essential discovery in 1666, it was not published until some sixteen years later. Historians dispute whether it was because Newton was using an inaccurate figure for the size of the earth, so that his early calculations came out a bit off, or whether it took him that time to satisfy himself that it was legitimate to idealize the earth as a single mass-point.

In any case, the insight was eventually revolutionary. It gave a theoretical explanation for Kepler's figures; and the law of gravitation was so powerful that astronomers, almost two hundred years later, analyzing the perturbations of the orbit of Uranus, successfully predicted the existence and position of Neptune. Thus deduction got the jump on observation.

Kekule

August Kekule (1829–96) is famous for his insight into the structure of the benzene ring, a basic chemical structure at the heart of a great many compounds. But explaining his insight will require a review of some basic chemistry.

Already in Kekule's time chemists realized that every element had a typical valence, which specifies the number of bonds of which the element is capable. Carbon is the element common to all of organic chemistry, and it has a valence of four: that is, it is capable of four bonds with other elements. Hydrocarbons, next, are combinations of carbon and hydrogen and hold an important place among organic compounds. The valence of the hydrogen atom is one, so it is capable of one bond.

The simplest arrangement of carbon and hydrogen, then, is a combination of one atom of carbon with four atoms of hydrogen. This is diagrammed as follows:

$$
\begin{array}{c}
\text{H} \\
| \\
\text{H}-\text{C}-\text{H} \\
| \\
\text{H}
\end{array}
$$

The chemical sign is CH_4, and this is the structure of methane, used to fuel the Bunsen burners in many chemistry labs; it is also called "swamp gas," because it arises naturally from decaying organic material.

The next simplest arrangement would, obviously, involve two carbon atoms. They would be bonded to one another as such: C-C. This means that each atom has one of its bonds occupied, and has three left. The resulting configuration is:

$$
\begin{array}{cc}
\text{H} & \text{H} \\
| & | \\
\text{H}-\text{C}-\text{C}-\text{H} \\
| & | \\
\text{H} & \text{H}
\end{array}
$$

and the chemical notation is C_2H_6; the name of the gas is ethane.

The next step in complexity involves three carbon atoms, bonded so: C-C-C. Clearly the middle atom has two bonds already occupied, while the end atoms have but one. This yields the following arrangement:

$$
\begin{array}{ccccccc}
& H & & H & & H & \\
& | & & | & & | & \\
H\!-\!\!\!&C&\!\!\!-\!\!\!&C&\!\!\!-\!\!\!&C&\!\!\!-\!H \\
& | & & | & & | & \\
& H & & H & & H &
\end{array}
$$

The chemical sign is C_3H_8, and the gas is propane.

The next step, of course, will involve four carbon atoms, which will result in

$$
\begin{array}{ccccccccc}
& H & & H & & H & & H & \\
& | & & | & & | & & | & \\
H\!-\!\!\!&C&\!\!\!-\!\!\!&C&\!\!\!-\!\!\!&C&\!\!\!-\!\!\!&C&\!\!\!-\!H \\
& | & & | & & | & & | & \\
& H & & H & & H & & H &
\end{array}
$$

This is C_4H_{10}, called butane.

By now the reader will have grasped the pattern. The fifth step is called pentane, C_5H_{12}.

$$
\begin{array}{ccccccccccc}
& H & & H & & H & & H & & H & \\
& | & & | & & | & & | & & | & \\
H\!-\!\!\!&C&\!\!\!-\!\!\!&C&\!\!\!-\!\!\!&C&\!\!\!-\!\!\!&C&\!\!\!-\!\!\!&C&\!\!\!-\!H \\
& | & & | & & | & & | & & | & \\
& H & & H & & H & & H & & H &
\end{array}
$$

The sixth step is hexane, or C_6H_{14}.

$$
\begin{array}{ccccccccccccc}
& H & & H & & H & & H & & H & & H & \\
& | & & | & & | & & | & & | & & | & \\
H\!-\!\!\!&C&\!\!\!-\!\!\!&C&\!\!\!-\!\!\!&C&\!\!\!-\!\!\!&C&\!\!\!-\!\!\!&C&\!\!\!-\!\!\!&C&\!\!\!-\!H \\
& | & & | & & | & & | & & | & & | & \\
& H & & H & & H & & H & & H & & H &
\end{array}
$$

This much was known at Kekule's time; but he was working with another compound, benzene, which had the notation C_6H_6. What would be its structure? It obviously has too few hydrogen atoms to conform to any of the foregoing diagrams. In fact, one notes an anomaly about it: the number of hydrogen atoms is exactly the same as that of the carbon atoms; whereas, in all the examples above, the number of hydrogen atoms is always twice the number of carbon atoms, plus two.

There is such a thing as a double carbon bond, and one can try that:

$$C=C=C=C=C=C$$

In this case, it is obvious that all the middle carbon atoms already have four bonds, so cannot take any hydrogen atoms; only the two end atoms have two free bonds, yielding:

$$\begin{array}{ccccc} H & & & & H \\ | & & & & | \\ C=C=C=C=C=C \\ | & & & & | \\ H & & & & H \end{array}$$

But this is C_6H_4, and Kekule was looking for C_6H_6.

Perhaps Kekule was at about this point with the problem, when, one night, he dreamt of a snake, biting its own tail. Strange as that may seem, it gave him the insight: the carbon atoms should be arranged, not in a line, but in a ring! This is usually diagrammed in hexagon form:

$$\begin{array}{ccc} & C \quad C & \\ C & & C \\ & C \quad C & \end{array}$$

Even this does not yield the solution immediately. If one joins the carbon ring with single bonds, one gets

Each carbon atom has two bonds, so could take two hydrogen atoms, yielding C_6H_{12}. On the other hand, double bonds yields

$$\text{hexagonal ring with all double bonds: } C=C, C, C, C=C$$

Since each carbon atom has four bonds, there is no room for hydrogen, so the formula would be C_6H_0. But Kekule may have felt he was getting closer now: his desired C_6H_6 is exactly half-way between the C_6H_{12} of the single bonds, and the C_6H_0 of the double bonds. The solution: alternate single and double bonds around the ring:

$$\text{hexagonal ring with alternating single and double bonds}$$

Each carbon atom, then, has two bonds on one side, and one on the other, for a total of three, leaving one free bond for hydrogen:

$$\text{benzene ring with H atoms attached to each carbon}$$

This remains the chemist's account of the structure of benzene and all its derivatives to this day, aside from some refining insights introduced by quantum mechanics.

Goodyear

Charles Goodyear (1800–1860) is very different from the men already considered. He was not at all a theoretician, but a cut- and-try man. His father owned a hardware store, and he had little more scientific education. But he is known for the invention of the vulcanization process for rubber, and the circumstances of his insight are of interest.

Rubber, in Goodyear's time, presented many problems in its natural state. It was runny in the summer, and turned brittle and cracked in the winter. Goodyear was convinced there must be some process which would make it a more suitable substance for practical use. Some of his predecessors had found promising results with nitrates, and then sulphur, but none was fully satisfactory.

Goodyear had spent years searching for an answer, had bankrupted the hardware business he had inherited, impoverished his sizable family, and still was obsessed with his quest. One day he was trying still another mixture of sulphur and rubber when his wife came to the door from the market. He had not expected her so soon, so surreptitiously he stuck the mixture in the oven and went out to meet her. Later he came back to retrieve the mixture and found, to his astonishment, that it had changed. It was more pliable, but had not melted in the heat; it held up under the test of cold as well. So that was the answer: sulphur plus heat! He named the process "vulcanization," after the god of the smithy, Vulcan.

What is notable here is the element of serendipity, already mentioned. Here it appears to take center stage: the breakthrough is almost entirely an accident. Nevertheless, such an insight is not altogether accidental; the result, however happenstance, can only be recognized by a person who is prepared for it; and that expectation is set by the question that had dominated Goodyear's days and nights for years. If his wife, for example, had discovered the pot, she would probably have thrown it out as just another of her husband's impractical messes.

It would be nice to report a happy ending to the story of Goodyear's assiduous quest, but in fact he spent the rest of his life fighting patent battles in the United States and Europe, and died $200,000 in debt. Perhaps his wife was right after all! Nevertheless, if history offers any consolation, Charles Goodyear's name is still attached to rubber products, while many of the solid burghers of his time, with far healthier bank balances, now lie forgotten completely.

Conclusion

The above accounts are not written for physicists, but for people of little or no background in science. No doubt a physicist or chemist would wince at the simplifications necessary to present these historic insights in an accessible way. But, should these pages happen to fall into the hands of scientists, the remedy is not far off. All they need to do is to note the refining and corrective insights that must be added to the above accounts. In doing so, they will learn much about the nature and occurrence of insight. For, again, the central interest here is not physics, or chemistry, but insight.

On the other hand, there may well be readers who have the opposite problem: the scientific examples, however simplified they may be, seemed far too difficult. They were doing fine in Plato's cave, in sports, and with jokes; but their eyes glaze over and their minds turn off when it comes to science, or they may experience a mental block when the discussion veers in any way towards mathematics. For such readers, three suggestions may be made.

The first is that almost everyone who has made an honest effort will have understood something of the foregoing. However minor that insight may seem, it is as good, for the purposes of analysis, as any other insight. The reader needs only identify that insight, then ask, How did it occur? What were the clues? What led to the breakthrough? How did it "feel" when I understood?

Next, even a failure to understand can be instructive. Readers might evaluate what they have understood, and what they have not. Then they may inquire, What would I need to grasp in order to understand this? Where was the author's presentation lacking? What clues did he leave out that would have allowed me to understand this? The insights resulting may be backward, or inverse, insights, but they too are perfectly adequate for analysis.

Finally, readers may reflect upon themselves as knowers. Why is it that mathematical and scientific materials stump me? What is it about my practical orientation that makes it very strange for me to think of spending years trying to figure out a process for altering rubber? Why do the theoretical pursuits of the scientists seem such an affront to my more common-sense approach? That will, in fact, be the question of the next chapter.

9

Common Sense and Science

In the preceding chapters various hints have been dropped regarding a difference between a common-sense and a scientific orientation, and it is time to pull them together into a clear pattern. For insights not only occur, they occur in typical contexts or recognizable procedures, which can themselves be understood. As early as the chapter on common-sense language for insight, it was noted that even common sense has some awareness of specialization of intelligence. With amusement, exasperation, or contempt, it is cognizant of the "nerd," the "wonk," the "ivory-tower specialist."

Well known is the story of Thales and the milkmaids. Thales was walking, so absorbed in his meditations on the stars that he fell into a well! The milkmaids saw it and laughed; how could anyone be so impractical as not to watch where he was going?

The Gospels reflect a similar contrast in the charming story of Martha and Mary:

> On their journey Jesus entered a village where a woman named Martha welcomed him to her home. She had a sister named Mary, who seated herself at the Lord's feet and listened to his words. Martha, who was busy with all the details of hospitality, came to him and said, "Lord, are you not concerned that my sister has left me to do the household tasks all alone? Tell her to help me."
>
> The Lord in reply said to her: "Martha, Martha, you are anxious and upset about many things; one thing only is required. Mary has chosen the better portion and she shall not be deprived of it" (Luke 10:38-41).

Insights evoke one another, as already noted, and common sense insights may merge, almost imperceptibly, into scientific insights. For example, the very down-to-earth, practical question of how to descend the ski slope in one piece led to an insight into inclined planes. The memory that Galileo had studied inclined planes might lead to an investigation of his discoveries; and soon one would be contemplating mathematical formulas relating time and distance for a ball descending an inclined plane.

But what is perhaps more notable than the movement from common-sense to scientific insights is the contrast between the two modes of understanding.

The Conan Doyle stories present it as a comparison between Watson and Holmes. Watson has written up the adventures of the detective, but Holmes complains that Watson has romanticized what should have been a matter of cold and unemotional science. It is like, Holmes concludes, mixing a love story with a proof from Euclid: the two move in entirely different realms, and should never be confused.

The same contrast may also be traced between Charles Goodyear and his wife. He is obsessed with a scientific quest, convinced there is some process that will render natural rubber practically usable, while his wife can only see the family business sliding into bankruptcy, and her husband, herself, and her children threatened with poverty and starvation.

Perhaps, in each of these cases, the deepest difference lies in the orientation or goal of the different mental activities. One might sum it up this way: the person of common sense understands to live; the scientist lives to understand. That was particularly so in the case of Holmes, who formulated the idea, it will be remembered, in so many words.

No doubt common sense is the prior orientation. It is concerned with the daily business of living. Quite possibly the first manifestation of human intelligence had to do with tool-making: how can this material be fashioned to achieve that practical end? As noted already, common-sense knowing feels little need for definitions; it has no theoretical pretensions. It desires to know only enough to get the job done.

The scientific orientation, on the other hand, implies a certain background of insights, because it is intelligence taking charge of its own program, and setting its own goals. The insight is achieved that intelligence is not only useful for living; it has its own vitality and thrust, and can set its own course. Very likely this development cannot take place until a society has achieved a certain level. A people completely taken up with the quest for survival are not likely to raise theoretical questions. There is need for that leisure the Greeks called *skole*; and probably also for a special class of people who enjoy that leisure and evince a penchant for thinking, for making insight not the helpful assistance to practical projects but an end in itself.

A difference between the two patterns should be noted. The common-sense orientation may be sufficient to itself, but the scientific pattern can never be more than a partial avocation. It is quite possible to imagine someone living a purely practical existence, and rarely or never bothering his or her head about definitions or theories. On the other hand, no one can live purely in the scientific pattern; there are little matters of eating and drinking, sleep and shelter, that will not go away, no matter how "brainy" a person may be. Even Holmes, who lived to think, liked to have fresh linen every day, including when he was living in a hovel on the moor. No doubt Jesus, Mary, and Martha all enjoyed the supper Martha was fixing. Newton, it is said, spent days and days at a time in his study, working on a difficult problem; but even he needed food placed at the door now and then. Goodyear, however absorbed he was in his researches, also needed occasionally to worry about groceries coming into the house.

The two orientations of intelligence are different enough as to be inclined toward a mutual suspicion and contempt. The attitude of common sense toward ivory-tower specialists has already been noted. The milkmaids ridiculed Thales; but he perhaps also pitied them for always looking at the ground, never thinking to gaze up at the stars, and wonder about them. Martha had little patience with her sister's involvement in an activity as impractical as conversation, and Goodyear's wife no doubt sometimes wished fondly that her husband were a bit more practical.

The scientific orientation sets up insight as a goal in its own right; in doing so, it fosters everything that leads to insight, and eschews whatever might distract. Watson found Holmes at times positively inhuman in his absorption in thought and his contempt for all else, while Holmes chided Watson for being romantic and unscientific.

A key moment in the breakthrough to science has already, in an earlier chapter, been recognized in the Greek achievement, and it may be helpful to examine that transition more closely. An initial element in the historic accomplishment is found in the search for definition. That may seem to be no great matter to those for whom the Greek insight has passed thoroughly into their common-sense tradition. One of the hoariest cliches for starting a talk is to say, Webster's Dictionary defines such and such a word in this way. Even practical people, in a discussion, may pause and say, "But how do you define . . ." whatever is the subject of the conversation. But here the disproportion of before and after enters in: what is perfectly obvious once the insight is achieved and communicated, was not at all so before it occurred.

This process may be followed with precision in the early Platonic dialogues. Socrates has had the insight; he knows what a definition is, in general. Even he does not appear to have the answer in most particular cases; but his interlocutors do not even, as yet, understand the question: they have not as yet had the requisite insight. The word *definition* does not exist, and the concept is not communicated widely in the common sense of the time; so Socrates tries, in this way and that, to communicate the insight he has had.

A good example is found in the *Laches*. Lysimachus is concerned about training his sons. Nicias and Laches, high-ranking military men, are called to assist; and so is Socrates. Socrates says he is willing to help, but points out there is a prior question: What are the boys being trained in? He suggests "virtue" as a general answer. It is rather silly to try to teach something unless one knows what it is, Socrates avers. "Then must we not first know the nature of virtue? For how can we advise anyone about the best mode of attaining something of whose nature we are wholly ignorant?" (133). That is hard to argue with.

Rather than tackle such a large subject, however, Socrates further suggests that they concentrate on one aspect of virtue, courage, with which the military men should be especially familiar. Thus is set the quest of the dialogue: What is courage? The question is easier to pose than answer. Laches begins by suggesting that courage is standing fast in the heat of battle. But that would not apply, Socrates points out, for the cavalryman, who must exhibit courage in motion. And what about courage off the battle field? Does not ordinary life often require courage? Gradually the idea dawns: Socrates is looking for a verbal formula that will apply to every instance of courage. "I was asking about courage and cowardice in general. And I will begin with courage, and once more ask what is that common quality, which is the same in all the cases, and which is called courage. Do you now understand what I mean?" (135).

Similarly, when Meno in the dialogue of that name gives many examples of virtue, Socrates insists: "Then do the same with the virtues. Even if they are many and various, yet at least they all have some common character which makes them virtues. That is what ought to be kept in mind by anyone who answers the question, What is virtue? Do you follow me?" (355). In the same way, Theaetetus offers many kinds of knowledge, but Socrates is searching for the underlying unity: "But the question you were asked, Theaetetus, was not, What are the objects of knowledge, nor yet how many sorts of knowledge there are. We do not want to count them, but to find out what the thing itself—knowledge—is. Is there nothing in that?" (851). In the *Euthyphro*, finally, Socrates asks the priest of that name to give him a definition of the holy: "Well, bear in mind that what I asked of you was not to tell me one or two out of all numerous actions that are holy; I wanted you to tell me what is the essential form of holiness which makes all things holy. I believe you held that there is one ideal form by which unholy things are all unholy, and by which all holy things are holy. Do you remember that?" (174).

Nicias and Laches—and Socrates, too, it turns out—have a common-sense knowledge of what courage is, because they have all experienced it in battle. They use the word volubly and correctly. So why is it that they—including Socrates—are perplexed when asked, "What is courage?" It is because they are being asked a new kind of question, not a common-sense question at all, but a scientific one. Up to this point, words have functioned to refer to things, practical things about which human activity has been concerned. But now, to answer Socrates' question, words will have to be turned on words themselves.

Words, then, will no longer be allowed to float with that amiable imprecision which is sufficient to common-sense purposes; they will be brought to heel, controlled, and determined to a precise, objective, and common meaning by the use of other words. That breakthrough may seem paltry, especially when Socrates himself fails to answer his own questions, What is love? What is knowing? But it quickly sets in motion other insights that will revolutionize human thought. Syllogism, for example, is a technique for control of logical thought. But the terms of a syllogism must be defined; and the middle term, particularly, must bear the same meaning each time it is used. Without the insight of definition, the syllogism is impossible; but once it occurs, within two generations, Aristotle has succeeded in codifying all the laws of logic.

Again, the syllogism makes possible the notion of science: a set of syllogisms so interlocked that each conclusion is grounded by its predecessors, with the whole founded in a small number of primary axioms that are self-evident. The best example of such a structure is Euclid's *Elements* of geometry. Both Watson and Holmes, it may be remembered, pointed to that ideal; and it is possible that Aristotle had that model in mind when he defined science in the *Posterior Analytics*.

What definition accomplishes is a certain objectivity. Until words are defined, discussants often talk past each other, because they mean different things by the same word. When the definition of words is agreed upon prior to a discussion, then there is a gain in mutual comprehension; at times, careful definition may even solve a disagreement; but at least it allows the controversy to be pursued more fruitfully.

That objectivity is rendered possible because definition moves from the particular to the general. The person of common sense is satisfied with particular cases: courage is standing fast in battle. The same person would probably have the nimbleness of mind to know how to use the word correctly in other circumstances. But the definition achieves a formula that applies universally to every relevant circumstance.

Once science sets its own program, definition quickly moves off into the abstract and theoretical. For example, Newton used the term "mass." What is mass? It is not quite the same as weight, because weight implies gravity. If a body is taken to the moon, it weighs less there, but its mass remains the same. That is why all the sciences develop their technical jargon, which may appear mere mystification to the person of common sense.

One meaning of the myth of the cave may be the journey from common sense to science. The cave dwellers of the story are the people of common sense, who see but the shadows of reality. They literally do not know what they are talking about, because they are unable to give definitions of the words they use. The one who is enlightened, on the other hand, is the one who is led to see things as they are in themselves, not in particular instances, but in the general case; he views, not their shadows, but their true nature and reality.

The mutual suspicion and incomprehension of common sense and science have already been noted; in Plato's myth they harden into hostility. The candidate for enlightenment is dragged, kicking and screaming, from the cave. When he returns from his scientific quest, he is ridiculed, because he has gotten "his eyes full of darkness." The cave dwellers are even anxious to kill anyone who would disturb their shadowy existence. And yet, Socrates and Glaucon agree, once a person has seen the light, he would have only contempt for the procedures and prizes of the dark cave; he would rather be the meanest of slaves than to return to such prescientific darkness.

But the last word should not go to hostility. Both common sense and science are fully human projects. Despite their difference in orientation, they share a common quest in insight. Abstruse scientists will always need persons of common sense to serve their practical needs. And science, though it appears to move off into the completely impractical, often returns—sometimes centuries later—with applications that turn out to be, after all, eminently practical. Anyone who drives to work on rubber tires, for example, has reason to be grateful for Goodyear's obsessive and seemingly impractical quest.

10

Retrospect

At times on a journey it is opportune to look back and assess the path that has been traveled. To this point attention has focused on insight; ensuing chapters will move on to other mental activities. Consequently it may be helpful to gather together what has been said about insight in the diverse contexts of common-sense language, sports, mystery stories, and science. The treatment will be organized under six headings: insight in itself, the "before" and "after" of insight, insights in relation to one another, inverse insights, common-sense insights, and scientific insights.

Insight in Itself

Insight is that mental (or inward) activity by which the mind grasps the intelligible connections between things that previously had appeared merely disparate. This act of understanding "sees" a pattern in data, where "seeing" is only a metaphor from physical sight. Sometimes referred to as the "Aha!" experience, it is often experienced as a sudden breakthrough.

Insight may happen quickly, "with the speed of thought"; as soon as one wonders about something, the answer comes. But other times it may arrive more slowly, as it did to Goodyear and Kekule.

In insight the mind is obviously at a high pitch of creative activity; yet there is another way in which, it was noted, insight is often experienced with a certain passivity: "it struck me," "it dawned on me," are common phrases. That is perhaps because insight is at once deliberately intended, and yet beyond specific control, as will be seen in the next chapter.

Memory was seen to play an important role in many insights: sometimes the insight grasps the relation between present circumstance and previously garnered information; sometimes the present insight is sparked by the memory of a past insight.

Trial and error were also seen to figure in many insights. Charles Good-year tried one thing after another until he found the right solution; a slip on the river bank forced a re-evaluation of how to walk a slope on ice-skates. Learning is not a process that leads purely and directly to the truth, but a self-correcting process that bumbles along many a by-path and dead-end until it finds the way out of the maze.

Insight was also seen to be abstractive. It catches the significant parallels between two situations while ignoring all else that is irrelevant. While it brings together the seemingly disparate into unity, it also leaves out of its purview what does not fit. If it sees a pattern, it also ignores what does not fit into the pattern. If it makes connections, it does not connect everything in some grand synthesis, but is satisfied with what has been achieved at the moment.

Insight was also seen to have a certain freedom in relation to its materials. Its prerequisites are more an inner readiness than an outer oc-casion. Many people had seen the lamp swing in the cathedral of Pisa, but only Galileo noted the peculiar relation between the times for swings of various widths. Many had seen an apple fall in an orchard, but only Newton grasped the law of universal gravitation.

Again, the same outer circumstance may ground different insights. The parents saw only hopelessness in their Christmas present; the boy saw only possibility. But as yet the "materials" of insight have not been iden-tified, and so this question is best put off to a later chapter.

The Disproportion of Insight in Prospect and Retrospect

An insight has been described as a breakthrough; once it occurs, the whole situation has changed. What first seemed puzzling now appears wonderfully coherent; aimless and unorganized details now fall into a beautiful unity; pattern appears where none was before; what was dis-parate is now connected.

That explains why there is such a contrast of "before" and "after" the insight. Before the insight occurs, the matter may seem a hopeless muddle, endlessly perplexing; but once the insight takes place, the whole seems very simple. That is why it is hard to realize, in reading Plato's dialogues, that once people did not understand what a definition was. Similarly, Wat-son speaks of "that constant and apparently purposeless series of small mysteries which had succeeded each other so rapidly. . . ." (696). Be-fore Holmes explained his deductions about the watch, Watson thought the detective had been investigating his brother's life; but afterward Watson concedes, "It is as clear as daylight" (93). Again, at the end of the Baskerville case Holmes summarizes well both the initial perplexity and the final clarity:

> The whole course of events, from the point of view of the man who called himself Stapleton, was simple and direct, although to us, who had no means in the beginning of knowing the motives of his actions and could only learn part of the facts, it all appeared exceedingly complex (761).

This characteristic of insight has implications for teaching, because the teacher stands across the divide of understanding from the pupil. What appears simple to the teacher, who has already grasped the point, leaves the pupil in a state of puzzlement. But the teacher has also been there, and can remember—perhaps dimly—being in a similar predicament. Even more importantly, the teacher has already made the transition from not understanding to understanding, and so is able to suggest clues, and point attention away from unrelated and distracting materials, so that the pupil too may have the experience of insight.

Insight is usually a relatively permanent acquisition. Once one has understood, that insight may usually be counted on as background for future learning. Even if one should forget how exactly it all fit together, the insight will normally occur much more easily the second time than the first.

What is true for the individual is also true for the society and the race. Thus the achievements and breakthroughs of one generation become the background insights of the next, allowing a constant forward progress. If this were not so, each generation would have to start from the same place, and the human race would never escape from the Stone Age. As Galileo put it with an appealing humility, "If we have seen far, it is because we have stood on the shoulders of giants."

Relation of Insights to One Another

Insights do not merely occur occasionally, in isolation; they are related one to another. As we have just seen, insights accumulate. They cohere with one another; they often evoke one another. One breakthrough occasions another, as Socrates' insight into definition allowed further insights into syllogism and the ideal of a science.

The most obvious example of this relationship has to do with refining insights, which "ride piggyback," as it were, on a main insight, to qualify it. So Galileo's rough-and-ready measure that the swing of a pendulum depends only on the length, even over a wide range of swings, was modified by later, more exact measurement. Another good example is found in chemistry with the gas laws. Boyle's law says that the volume of a gas is inversely proportional to its pressure. For example, if the volume of a gas is doubled (while the temperature is held constant), its pressure will be halved. That gives good enough results in many cases, but it is not quite accurate. It is based on an ideal gas, whose atoms are points with no size, and which have no attraction for one another. A chemist by the name of van der Waals modified Boyle's law to allow for these two factors, thus yielding the more refined van der Waals's formula. But even this is not equal to all circumstances, and so still more elaborate equations have been worked out.

Perhaps most important, insights may grasp other insights, see how they fit together, note how the individual patterns they discover can connect into ever-larger patterns. Jokes were seen often to be structured, for example, as an insight that grasped two other insights and their mutual incomprehension. And to understand that requires a fourth insight, which understands the three insights in their respective relationships.

The process would appear to have no built-in limits. As one ascends a mountain, one comes to higher and higher viewpoints, by which one sees more and more comprehensively where one has been. The same can be said of mental achievement, which also provides its higher viewpoints, where previous achievements, once grasped as disparate, now fall into an overarching unity, as present insight organizes past insights into unity. A good example is found in Newton, whose single insight into the relation of distance and mass organized and gave coherent explanation to vast ranges of observations on the paths of the known planets, and yet remained so unexhausted that it also predicted the existence of a planet not yet observed.

The goal of this chapter is even more ambitious, for it is trying to synthesize and bring into unity a set of insights about all potential insights— something like a definition which, as Socrates said, applies universally to every instance. To the extent that these insights are correct, they describe all insights, those that have been specifically analyzed, all those from the past that they represent as having a similar structure, and even— presuming that the human mind will continue to function in the future as it has in the past—all those that ever will take place.

Inverse Insight

Reference has been made here and there in the preceding pages to a backward, or inverse, insight. It will be worthwhile to try to define that paradoxical notion more accurately. The inverse insight grasps that, contrary to all expectations, there is nothing to be understood in a particular situation or question. It is not a simple failure to understand, but a positive grasp; yet the grasp is to the effect that the situation is unintelligible. To put it another way, an inverse insight grasps at once a situation, a question, and the fact of an incommensurability between the two. An inverse insight, then, grasps not what is right with the answer, but what is wrong with the question.

"What is the difference between a chicken?" The person to whom this riddle is posed sees immediately that there is no answer to such a question; rather the question itself is illegitimate, ill-formed. In the riddle about the elephant in the refrigerator, similarly, one understands immediately the incongruity of the whole idea, which the "answer" only underlines. Other jokes were seen to function in the same way: the story line created one set of expectations, only to have them dashed by the surprise ending (e.g., the shirt salesman having the answer, when all the medical experts failed).

Such examples are trivial, and may lead one to wonder why such a fuss is being made over inverse insight; but other inverse insights, especially in science, are significant indeed. Anyone approaching the swinging lamp in the cathedral of Pisa would be inclined to ask—and it was perhaps Galileo's original question—"How does the timing of the swings vary as their height gradually decays?" But the answer is, it doesn't vary. So the insight of Galileo is into the non-importance of the width-of-the-swing element, which invalidates and corrects the original question.

The same is even more true with Newton's first law of motion. To the ordinary person, a state of rest and a state of motion seem like very different things. That things at rest tend to stay at rest, unless something moves them, is obvious enough; but the idea that what is in motion tends to stay in exactly the same motion, unless acted on by an outside force, appears counter to experience. What Galileo and Newton grasped, however, is that, once one abstracts from friction, rest and motion are essentially the same; that under their apparent difference is an underlying similarity, which confers a satisfying unity on the laws embracing both motion and rest, where rest is merely a special case in which velocity is zero. Without that insight, the breakthrough under the apple tree would have been impossible.

Common-Sense Insight

Since this topic received extended attention in the last chapter, it will suffice to make three summary points.

The first is that insight is very much a part of common-sense knowing. One does not have to be a scientist to have insights! Even a joke, it was seen, can involve a fairly sophisticated pattern of insights.

Second, common sense is not unaware of insight. It does not, of course, attempt to define it, and its theoretical interests in the subject are strictly limited; yet it possesses a shrewd grasp of what it is to understand or to fail to understand, to understand readily and to be slow to get the point. There is even a limited awareness that insight functions in different patterns, and that common sense has no monopoly—though this concession may be grudging—on modes of understanding.

For common sense, finally, is eminently and rigorously practical. It is, like Martha, busy about many things. The world's work is waiting to be done, and common sense fails to see how strange questions like, What is courage? What is love? What is knowing? will be of much help.

Scientific Insight

At some point, however, mind becomes aware of itself, and not just the "outer" world that it knows. Then what has been merely a means of intelligent practice can become an end: as if a horse, who normally works in the fields, is suddenly allowed to run free in a pasture; or a car that has been used for daily commuting is taken on the open road. What will it do if the accelerator is pushed all the way to the floor?

What intellect does, when given its own head, is, first, to assemble its tools. One of those tools is words, and so words are turned upon words to create precise definitions. This allows the more sophisticated use of logic. All of Aristotle's logical works, taken together, are referred to as the *organon*—which literally, and quite appropriately, means "tool." Finally, intelligence establishes its own ideal in the notion of "science." As Aristotle defines it in the *Posterior Analytics*, science is "certain knowledge through causes."

The move from common sense to science, then, is a move from the subjective to the objective. It seeks to replace various subjective meanings of words with one commonly agreed-upon definition. It is a movement from the personal to the impersonal. That is why Holmes wanted to dissociate detection from feeling: it must be coldly scientific, not skewed by any personal prepossessions or arbitrary emotions. Ultimately, the knower tends to become the instrument of a scientific project larger than himself, rather than intellect being a tool of his more egotistical needs. The move is one from the particular to the general. Definition seeks an expression of the universal case, and scientific laws aim always toward larger and larger generality. Finally, the movement is from the sensible to the supra-sensible. The notion of weight, of what "feels heavy," is transmuted into "mass," a theoretical construct at home in the depths of the oceans, at the top of a mountain, on the moon, or even in the weightlessness of space. Chains are idealized into lines of infinite thinness, and the earth is conceived of as a single point-mass—abstract ideas which have never been experienced. Kekule speaks authoritatively on the structure of the benzene ring, which no one has ever seen, because atoms and molecules are far too small to see. Science moves, often with bewildering rapidity, from the familiar world of sights, sounds, and tactile impressions into a highly recondite world of theoretical constructs and mathematical formulas.

11

Question, Inquiry, and the Heuristic

Insight is the central act of mental process, but not the only one; the focus must shift now to what immediately precedes insight. A clue may be taken from Sherlock Holmes who, in solving the Baskerville case, was seen to move from question to suspicions to insight. Our examination will move from the question to the tension of inquiry to the heuristic.

The Question

Insights are preceded by questions, and questions are therefore crucial to having insights. It has been noted that many people shared the experience of Galileo in the cathedral of Pisa, and many the experience of Newton in the orchard. What made the difference was the question. Only Galileo wondered about the law of the pendulum; only Newton wondered about the law of gravitation. Without those questions, neither Galileo nor Newton would have been wiser than anyone else.

Questions are so important that they have already, willy-nilly, entered into the discussion. In chapter 3 it was asked, What is metaphor? What is nimbleness of mind? The question of the detective story, it was seen in chapter 6, is popularly expressed as "whodunit?" Chapter 7, on humor, noted that questions can carry presuppositions; in the following chapter, Goodyear's obsessive question was seen to dominate years of research. Chapter 9 offered examples of two orientations toward insight, then asked, What is the contrast? Theoretical questions like, What is courage? What is virtue? What is mass? were seen to have different preoccupations than the more usual common-sense questions. Chapter 10, finally, in its reflection on the inverse insight, revealed the possibility of an ill-formed question.

What, then, is a question? (As Socrates turned words on words, it may be noted in passing, here question is being turned on question.) The question is such a basic mental reality that it is hard to define. But we can say that it is that mental activity which focuses a more general interest or curiosity. It initiates a search for an answer, which will be successfully concluded when the relevant insight has occurred.

The Tension of Inquiry

Auguste Rodin created a statue entitled "The Thinker." A man is seated on a stone. His elbow rests on his knee, and his chin on his clenched fist. He stares into the mid-distance, but it is obvious that his focus is not so much "outer" as "inner."

For a more homey example, think of a father helping a son with his homework. "Think!" the father urges. What is he asking the son to do? The son may throw out an answer at random, and the father will insist, "You're just guessing. Try to think, for goodness sake!"

A question may lead to an answer with the speed of thought, but it may be that a discrete time will intervene; then the question creates an intellectual tension. The mind has grasped the question. It searches for the answer. It tries to eliminate distractions, and to concentrate its attention. It tries to recall memories that might be appropriate, or perhaps a process that has been used successfully in the past. Can logic be of help? I know this; what does it imply? I know that; if I combine the two facts, what do they tell me?

Both Watson and Holmes were in that precise state of mind at the beginning of the Baskerville case. As Watson described it: "Holmes sat in silence as we drove back to Baker Street, and I knew from his drawn brows and keen face that his mind, like my own, was busy in endeavoring to frame some scheme into which all these strange and apparently disconnected episodes could be fitted." It may not be accident that both "The Thinker" and Holmes are pictured seated, because the bodily repose allows full scope to the mind. Both are in silence, because conversation would be distracting. Holmes's "drawn brows" and "keen face" are witness to the mental effort going on within.

This process from question to insight is not without a sense of movement. Holmes is clearly closing in on an insight when he says, early in the Baskerville affair, "The thing takes shape, Watson. It becomes coherent." We also saw that Kekule, examining the possibilities of single and double bonds in the carbon ring, may have felt he was moving closer to a solution. When we were children, we played a search game, where one person did the searching and the others encouraged him, "You're getting warmer! You're getting colder!" Something like that takes place in intellectual searches. One does not know the answer yet—else the search would be over. But one feels sure it is "just around the corner."

When the answer finally does come, it is experienced as a release; and the greater the tension has been, the more prolonged the inquiry, the greater that release will be. Teachers are familiar with it: they observe some students smile with the satisfaction of having found the answer, while others continue to frown in concentration. Perhaps the most striking instance of the excitement of the release of insight in the history of science is in the story about Archimedes. He had been posed a difficult question by the king: a crown had been prepared for him—but was it genuine gold, or an alloy? "Find out—but don't mar the crown in any way!" After days of pondering the problem, Archimedes took some time off to relax. As he settled into the baths of Syracuse, he suddenly saw the answer: "Submerge the crown in water to determine its specific gravity!" Without bothering to put on his clothes, he ran into the streets, naked, shouting "Eureka! Eureka!" "I've found it!"

The Heuristic

The Greek word Archimedes used, *heurisko* (in the present tense), finds an echo in the English *heuristic.* Lonergan uses the word to describe the strategy of moving from question to insight. For there is a strange paradox to the process of inquiry: one has not yet understood, obviously, or one would not be searching; yet the search is not simply unknowing, or uninformed, but intelligent.

A computer may be set to solve a problem by "brute force," by going through all the logical possibilities until the correct one is found. Whether there are thousands of possibilities or millions doesn't matter, as long as each operation can be done quickly enough. But human beings do not usually search so blindly. Even Goodyear, a "cut-and-try" man if there ever was one, did not choose his materials at random; he was working with sulphur because it had already produced promising results.

Though intelligent, however, the search for insight is not governed by specific rules. If it were, the process would become quasi-automatic, and computers could be programmed to make great scientific discoveries. Insight can come through hunches, inspired guesses, or educated estimations; through serendipitous connections, chance experiences, or knowing what to look for when the accidental has occurred. For Kekule, the basic insight came in sleep, showing that even the subconscious goes to work on a problem, throwing up the images that will yield the insight.

Common sense is content to word its questions in the familiar what, who, when, where, why, and how. Socrates still uses that common-sense language in addressing to his pre-scientific colleagues such questions as, What is virtue? What is knowing? But already he can be seen moving toward a more scientific procedure when he asks, What is the nature of courage? What is the universal form of the holy?

Science, as it seeks exact definition of its terms, also attempts to systematize the process from question to insight. So the mathematician will call the unknown quantity he is looking for "x." The procedure is then to list everything known about "x." With sufficient manipulation, this is usually sufficient to assign a specific value to "x."

The physicist has a similar heuristic procedure, but uses "nature." What is the nature of free fall? What is the nature of pendicular movement? What is the nature of gravity? The botanist will ask, What is the nature of the live oak? the slash pine? The geologist will ask, What is the nature of clay? of quartz? The question, of course, does not immediately supply the answer; usually investigation and measurement will still be required. But the intelligence of the search is not left quite so much to chance or hunch; it has received a more systematic form that will become a standard part of scientific procedure.

Questions have their presuppositions, we noted when speaking of jokes; but the same is true in science. All things being equal, the more background insights one brings to an investigation, the more quickly one will come to insight. But those background insights also carry with them presuppositions and expectations, which can prove an obstacle rather than a help. At times a field is ripe for a radical shift of perspective. Then a young person, who can absorb quickly the state of the question, but be free enough of settled procedures to grasp quite new perspectives, may be the person best situated to have the insight. One thinks of Thomas Aquinas at the age of nineteen, studying the work of Aristotle at the University of Naples, and grasping the possibility of a whole new synthesis of Christian philosophy and theology. Galileo was only seventeen when he measured the swinging lamp with his pulse at Pisa, and Newton was only twenty-four when he had his key insights at Woolsthorpe. Einstein worked out the ideas of special relativity while working in the patent office at Bern by the age of twenty-six; and P. A. M. Dirac had made some of his basic contributions to quantum mechanics by the time he was twenty-four.

Conclusion

It may be timely to remind the reader that the journey being proposed is both an inner and a personal one. The goal here is not merely to gather an extensive list of the abstract properties of insight, or the stages from question to insight, but to have readers identify them, as much as possible, in their own conscious experience. What has been said now about the process of inquiry may allow a better specification of the conditions of that personal identification.

At the end of the chapter on scientific insights we noted that our examples might have been at once too simplified for scientists, and too difficult for others. The fact is, each reader is different. What is child's play for one may be impossibly difficult for another. Neither of these levels of difficulty will be of much help in a personal experience of insight. If the insight comes too quickly, one does not experience the tension of inquiry, the searching which is neither completely systematic nor altogether unintelligent, the release of insightful breakthrough. On the other hand, if the material is too hard, one experiences the tension, but it ultimately turns to frustration rather than release. The answer, obviously, is for each reader to find some mid-level of difficulty, a question or problem that is challenging, without being impossible or beyond one's powers.

Two activities have now been identified, the question for understanding and the insight, and this will furnish the beginning of a structure to be gradually assembled. Taking a tip from the ascent in the myth of the cave, these activities will be listed from bottom to top:

> Insight
> Question for Understanding

12

Conception and the Concept

In the joke about the foreigner and his wife we mentioned that "inconceivable" is usually taken as an intellectual metaphor. The time has come to focus on the mental activity named "conception."

Some prior attention, however, must be given to the way the world is typically given to us in experience. Georges Seurat was a painter of the impressionist period who developed a style of painting called pointillism, and a theory about colors to go along with it. In what he saw as a scientific approach to aesthetics, he held that the painting should consist of many tiny points of diverse color, which would then blend into the correct impression on the eye at a certain distance. Anyone who has examined closely "Sunday Afternoon on the Island of La Grande Jatte" is familiar with these small points and their effect.

Seurat's theory may recall the work of Kekule, which also had to do with atoms and molecules, the building blocks of matter. The idea, in fact, is not a new one: already among the Greeks Democritus taught that all matter is composed of tiny atoms.

Whatever the truth of these Greek and modern theories, it remains that they are scientific elaborations; they do not reflect the way people originally experience the world. While it may be theoretically appealing to think we encounter first atoms, then molecules, then cells, then living things, each built up out of the previous, smaller elements, in fact we first experience the world in "globs" or "units," and only then, perhaps, reason back to the tinier atoms from which they are constructed.

Probably the first reality the infant separates out from its surrounding environment is its parents. Other living creatures may then attract recognition: a brother or sister, a pet cat or dog. A dog may at first be called a "bow-wow," for the units that are recognized have characteristics.

A further step is necessary. The larger units of experience tend to be repeated. Imagine now a child a little older, say, a four-year-old, on the train with its mother. The mother points out an animal in a pasture and says, "Look—there's a cow!" Shortly after, it will be the child saying, "Look, Mom—a cow!"

Note that the understanding that links the two cows under the same name is a spontaneous process. The mother does not say, "Johnny—there's a cow. Now in life you will experience other sensations similar to this one, and then you may again legitimately use the same word 'cow' to apply to them too." The facts that the world is experienced in units, and that those units tend to be repetitious, would appear almost instinctive with the human mind.

Were this not the case, the world of experience would be almost unknowable, unorganizable. Each time we encountered another animal, for example, we would have to find a new name for it; and nothing learned in previous encounters would be applicable to the present one. Conversely, the experience of the world as a series of repetitious units with stable characteristics means a vast speeding up of the learning process, because whatever is learned about one particular unit can be applied to any other of the same type.

Conception, then, is the mental activity that explicitly expresses this generality. The mind produces a concept, which formulates that generality; and it is this concept which is betokened by a general word such as "cow."

Insight, as already noted, grasps a certain generality. But the insight is an understanding of a particular situation; a certain universality is already implied in it, but it takes the concept to formulate that universality explicitly, as such. The insight, then, is a grasp of the universal-in-the-particular; the concept expresses the universal as such.

The definition and the concept can then be seen as closely related. The definition is a verbal formulation that indicates the extension of the concept. When Socrates asked, "What is courage?", he might have asked, "What is the concept of courage?" In other words, "What is that universal core that is present in every particular understanding of an instance of courage?"

Similarly, science and the concept are closely connected. Socrates' very attempt to formulate definitions was an initial move into science. What is expressed in the concept is the sole interest of science, because it seeks to formulate general laws. This does not mean that concepts do not occur in common-sense usage. Even a four-year-old can use a concept accurately. But common sense remains vitally interested in the particular, whereas science moves off to the universal: it does not want to know merely this hydrogen atom, this frog, this cow, but general natures, so that its knowledge will be applicable wherever in the universe those natures occur. Not surprisingly, Aristotle defined the object of science in the *Posterior Analytics* as "the universal and the necessary." Otherwise, again, the learning process would be critically hobbled, because a different science would have to be worked out in every particular place and time, with the results to be shared by no one. Scientific progress would grind to a halt.

Concept and formulation are also closely tied together. When a general reality is conceived, it can be readily expressed; but without a concept, expression is halting and round-about, at best. Eskimos, it is said, have many more words for "snow" than other people do. There are words for "icy snow," "wind-packed snow," and so on. Other people may have experienced the same conditions, but not often enough to notice regularities. Or perhaps the experience is simply not intrusive enough, or important enough for survival, to bother formulating. (Skiers, however, are aware of the way snow can modulate from a crisp, groomed surface in the early morning to a soft, slushy surface at midday on an early spring day; and they speak of "powder," "deep powder," "packed powder," "ice," "granular snow," and "corn snow.")

Identifying the Activity of Conception

Catching the mind in the act of conceiving is not as easy as recognizing an insight. The question or problem may be varied in difficulty, as already seen, so that some lapse of time may exist between the question and the solution that releases the tension of inquiry. Conception, however, as mentioned, is a quasi-instinctive mental process, and it is not so easy to imagine a situation in which one understands, but has enough difficulty formulating that understanding universally so that the process might be recognized. Nevertheless, it may be helpful to take a couple of stabs at it.

A person understands something as personal. Later on, that person may come to realize that this very personal understanding may have relevance to other persons' experience as well. Perhaps that second moment is the production of the concept?

The tension of the particular and the general has revealed itself quite clearly in the history of the science of psychology. Psychology is a strange kind of science. Sigmund Freud, the founder of modern psychology, always asserted strongly that—like Holmes!—he was a scientist. But he complains bitterly in the preface to *The Interpretation of Dreams* that other scientists have not taken him seriously. The reason was perhaps that botanists study trees and astronomers study stars, but the psychologist studies—the psychologist! Carl Jung faces the quandary in the early pages of his *Memories, Dreams, Reflections*—his autobiography cannot be scientific, because he is an individual, and there is no science of the individual, only of the general.

Carl Rogers, in *On Becoming a Person*, formulates the same tension in another way. He espoused "soft data"—people's subjective accounts of their experience, including his own—as well as the "hard data" which came from statistics or animal studies. To use the terminology developed here, he valued "inner" as well as "outer" data. But he did so with misgivings, because he knew that many other scientists would not approve—as Freud had painfully learned. So he presented his findings cautiously and tentatively. What he found, however, was that his audiences responded enthusiastically, with recognition. In time, he came to formulate this as a law: What is most personal is also most universal.

To return to the question of conception, the suggestion is that Rogers had an insight when he first understood something about himself; he had the corresponding concept when he realized the universal implications of that personal understanding. The example, however, is open to an objection: Does a new insight intervene when Rogers grasps that his personal experience may have relevance for other persons?

Another example may be drawn from the connection of concept and formulation. Are there times when we understand, but are unable to formulate what we have understood—suggesting that the insight is present, without a concept?

That people sometimes have difficulty formulating their thought is certainly true. But that is, at least sometimes, a sign that understanding has not yet taken place. Teachers use a criterion: "If you can't explain it in your own words, then you haven't really understood it."

Another possibility is that the insight may be so tied to the conditions of particularity that it has no universal formulation. An example would be the artist. Scientific pretensions aside, the artist has an insight (a real intellectual activity, not simply an emotion) but expresses it in a work of art, not in a concept. It is not that the artist is slow to articulate the concept, formulating it after the painting or sculpture is completed. The artist who can articulate the insight functions at that moment not as an artist, but as an art critic. The critic does attempt to formulate the meaning of the work. But two things should be noted: to those outside the art world, those formulations often seem very opaque; and even the critic who succeeds in being crystal clear remains an accessory-after-the-artistic-fact: no one would think of substituting such prose in a museum for the original work of art.

Do there remain, then, general conceptions of insights that can be consciously distinguished from the insights themselves? This, as one of the finer points of cognitional process, will be left as an open question.

The three activities of questioning, understanding, and conceiving Lonergan groups together as the unitary level of understanding.

	Concept
Level of Understanding	Insight
	Question

13

Misunderstanding and the Reflective Question

Besides the lack of understanding, which is a simple failure to have an insight, and the inverse insight, which is a grasp that there is nothing to be understood, there is also misunderstanding, which is an insight that does not get it right. Most of the examples given of insight, naturally enough, have stressed accurate insights. But misunderstanding was clear in some of the jokes: the piano player, for example, misunderstood the question of the patron, and the dinner guests misunderstood what the flustered woman was referring to. If these misunderstandings were trivial and comic, they can also be more tragic. Think of the ending of *Romeo and Juliet*. Romeo sees the drugged Juliet, and understands her to be dead; he kills himself, which she discovers when she awakes. Insights, then, can be accurate understandings, or they can be mere "bright ideas" that do not work out in practice. Insight, therefore, is not the terminus of the intellectual process, but leads to a further question: Is the insight true? This is the question for reflection.

The question for reflection differs from the question for understanding in that its appropriate answer is a mere yes or no. The question for understanding, as seen already, inquires who, what, when, where, why, or how. The proper answer is a person, a thing, a place, a time, a cause, or a method. But the question for reflection follows upon such an answer, and asks, is it so? The appropriate answer is yes or no. For example, if Galileo asks, What is the nature of the pendulum's movement? the proper answer is some functional relationship between the width of the swings, and the time the pendulum takes to complete a period. To such a question it would make no sense to answer yes or no. But once Galileo has the insight that the time remains constant, the reflective question becomes appropriate: Does the time of the period actually remain stable over a wide variety in the amplitude of the swings? Here the only proper response is yes or no.

To concretize the notion of the question for reflection, some examples may now be given: again common-sense situations will be stressed. Imagine a husband and wife about to leave on a vacation. He asks her, "Have you turned off the furnace? Locked the doors?" This is a question for reflection, because he is not asking where the furnace switch is, or what kind of bolts are on the doors; he does not expect an explanation of pilot lights or a disquisition on dead-bolts, but a simple yes or no.

A doctor is speaking to a patient. "This could be a case of a pinched nerve. We will have to run a test to find out." Implicit here is the reflective question, "Is this really a case of a pinched nerve?"

A woman tells a detective. "I think my husband is having an affair." What is taking place here is an insight, perhaps based on a number of clues. But the woman is asking the detective to investigate and gather evidence to decide whether or not the insight is true. The reflective question implied is, Is my husband really having an affair or not?

A young man sits picking petals off a daisy. "She loves me . . . she loves me not. . . ." The question that may be implicit in his mind is, Does she truly love me, or not?

A young girl is walking with her mother through snow-filled woods. "Is each snowflake really different from every other one?" she asks. That, too, is a question for reflection.

Hamlet tries to decide whether or not his uncle has killed his father. He understands that this could be so, and he has some clues. But he needs to be sure. The traveling players offer him the opportunity: "The play's the thing / Wherein I'll catch the conscience of the king." Implicit here is the question, Did my uncle really kill my father?

If the question for reflection may be implicit in some common-sense situations, ordinary language also has ways to underline the question. Imagine the same husband and wife on a further leg of their vacation. She asks him, "Are you sure we're on the right train?" The "Are you sure?" makes very explicit that this is a question for reflection. One might also ask, "Is it true that you once had a nervous breakdown?" More professorial types are wont to ask, "Is it the case that . . .?" Here we see not merely a question for reflection, but a certain awareness of it as such even in common-sense language.

Work teams or planning committees will have "brainstorming sessions." These are understood, more or less explicitly, as times to produce insights at all costs, without worrying for the moment about the reflective question. Later, it is understood, the ideas produced will have to be examined more soberly; bright but ideal dreams will have to be separated from concrete possibilities; details of proposals will have to be worked out; data may need to be investigated; in short, some "reality check" will have to be imposed. The question for reflection is not eliminated, only deliberately postponed.

Mathematics has an explicit way of speaking about this process: it is called "checking." One multiplies 38 by 46 to get 1748. The reflective question supervenes: Is that product correct? Normally one checks by reversing the process, dividing 1748 by 46. If 38 is the result, then one can be sure the product is correct.

Insights can concern not merely past or present fact, but future performance. Here the question for reflection becomes particularly sensitive. Imagine a homeowner speaking to a contractor who is to do some home repairs. "I understand completely your good intentions; but how can I be sure you will carry them out?" The homeowner is saying in effect, "You have led me to an insight into a future possibility. But there is still the question for reflection: Is this insight accurate?" Many sadder but wiser homeowners could offer a long commentary on the importance of the question for reflection, even though they might not recognize the term.

Again, think of the bank loan officer speaking to a loan prospect. "You tell me that you can afford to pay back the loan on time. But how can I be sure? What collateral do you have to offer?"

The question for reflection, then, marks a shift in the knowing process. Attention turns from understanding to the accuracy, sureness, and certainty of understanding. Thus the reflective question introduces a new level of cognitional process:

Level of Reflection	Question for Reflection
	Concept
Level of Understanding	Insight
	Question for Understanding

14

Judgment

The judgment is the mental activity that provides the answer to the question for reflection. In its briefest expression, that is a simple yes or no. But it may always be filled out by reference to the question for reflection. "Yes, I turned off the furnace." "No, I'm not really sure this is the right train." "Yes, your husband is, I'm afraid, having an affair."

Judgment may then be compared and contrasted with insight. Both are answers to questions: the insight to the question for understanding, the judgment to the question for reflection. But this difference should also be noted: the concept that formulates the insight may be expressed in a word; the insight may be summarized in a phrase; but the judgment always requires a proposition. It affirms that something is, that a state of affairs truly obtains, that X is really Y. Even when it is expressed elliptically—as in a child saying, "Look, Mom, a cow!"—it may be filled out: "[That is] a cow!"

What sets judgment off from all prior mental activities is that it stands for a personal commitment. With the judgment, one is no longer merely defining, supposing, imagining, or brainstorming: one is taking a personal stance ("It is the case that . . .").

One might think of the metaphor of playing chess. As long as one keeps one's finger on the piece to be moved, one is only examining options, looking at possible future moves. But once one moves a piece and takes one's finger off, one is committed. Similarly, as long as one is understanding, brainstorming for new ideas, checking the process, considering the question for reflection, one is not yet committed. But once one pronounces a judgment, one's integrity is at stake.

That is why people usually do not like to be told that they are wrong. They will not be embarrassed to forget something—anyone can have trouble remembering—but they can be counted on to be unhappy if their statement is proved wrong. Often they will seek an excuse. In the most blatant cases, they may deny ever making the statement. If given proof that they did make the affirmation, they may try to diminish their responsibility. "I don't remember saying that; and if I did, perhaps I was joking." "I must have been dreaming when I said that." "It was a slip of the tongue." "I was under the influence of drugs or alcohol." "My captors forced me to say it." Often a person will search for euphemisms: "I misspoke myself." "I may have given a misleading impression."

The reason that persons are responsible for their judgments is because—as opposed to the simplified presentation given so far—judgments are not limited to a simple yes or no. There are also probable judgments, with an almost infinite number of degrees in between. "Yes, I'm almost sure I locked all the doors." "That appears to me to be highly probable." "That may or may not be the case." "There is a 20 percent chance of rain tomorrow." "It's possible, but, I would say, highly unlikely." "I don't think so—but never say never!" Not only are there probable judgments, but one can withhold judgment. "I have an open mind; I'm waiting for all the evidence to come in." "I'm not ready as yet to pronounce judgment on that." "Give me a week to think that over—I'm still not sure."

Can judgments be identified in common-sense language? In fact, they are everywhere. If one leaves aside questions, exclamations, commands, and wishes, then practically all of human discourse, whether spoken or written, is composed of judgments.

Common sense not only makes judgments, it is aware of making them. Two boys arguing with each other—"Are too!" "Am not!" "Are too!" "Am not!"—underline judgment by repetition and opposition. People say, "I told you so!" "You assured me of that, and now events have proved you wrong." "You knew that wasn't true even as you were saying it, you liar!"

As questions for reflection can concern the future, so can judgments. "I'll meet you tomorrow." "I promise this will arrive overnight." Sometimes the element of personal responsibility appears to be deliberately highlighted. "Take my word for it—it ain't gonna happen!" "I know, because I've been there."

The same element is even more formally stressed in an oath. "I swear to tell the truth, the whole truth, and nothing but the truth, so help me God." "I take you for better or for worse, in sickness and in health, until death do us part."

As insight can happen with the quickness of thought, so may judgment. The child who exclaims, "Look, Mom, a cow!" is not aware of understanding that what he is seeing corresponds to the concept "cow," and that he is answering the implicit question for reflection, "Is that really a cow?" But there are other cases where a period of time clearly intervenes between the question for reflection and the judgment. Think of a judge saying, "The question before the court is, Did this man commit the crime of which he is accused? I have now heard all the evidence; I will deliver my verdict next Tuesday." (Note that "judge" and "judgment" have both an ordinary and a technical meaning. Nor is that an accidental coincidence, for the judge does more formally what the person of common sense does in every judgment.)

The lapse of time may be particularly evident in science. There an investigator may propose an hypothesis that may require years, even decades, to vindicate. Sixteen years elapsed between Newton's original conception of the law of gravity and his publication of it. It may even happen that the original researcher dies, and it falls to his successors to provide compelling proof for his tentative assertions.

In sum, judgment is a mental act that takes place on the level of reflection, as the response to a question for reflection. It affirms something to be the case, or that an assertion is true. Always it involves a commitment; to a greater or lesser extent, one's personal integrity is at stake in every judgment.

	Judgment
Level of Reflection	Question for Reflection
	Concept
Level of Understanding	Insight
	Question for Understanding

15

Reflective Insight

What mediates between the question for reflection and the judgment? To use the example of the last chapter, what will the judge do between the day he announces that he has heard all the evidence and the following Tuesday, when he promises to render a verdict? He will weigh the evidence. As it happens, this metaphor is nicely symbolized by the figure of Justice holding a set of scales. But what the judge does formally as an exercise of his office, the person of common sense does more spontaneously. What mental activity, then, does "weighing the evidence" signify?

To weigh the evidence and to arrive at a grounded judgment is to come to an understanding, but an understanding on the reflective level, one that grasps the sufficiency of evidence for making the judgment. The question for reflection asks, Is this proposition true? The reflective insight grasps the sufficient weight of evidence for the proposition. The judgment then affirms the proposition.

Common-sense language shows some familiarity with this aspect of mental activity. "You're jumping to conclusions!" someone might say. That means, in more formal terms, you are making judgments without properly and carefully weighing the evidence first. Again, one might hear, "That's a very serious accusation you are making; can you offer any proof for it?" This means, proper evidence must be supplied for the judgment. The businessman might say, "All right, what are the pros and cons of the Talbot deal?" He is asking for a weighing of the evidence for and against the proposition, This prospective sale will be good for the company. Similarly a person of common sense may formalize somewhat a difficult decision by listing on two sides of a page all the pros and cons. Still again, one hears people say, "That's a judgment call," when the weight of the evidence is not immediately apparent; and it will take further consideration, and perhaps a person with a specialized background, to see in which direction the evidence points.

What common sense does more or less spontaneously, geometry takes particular pains to formalize. "Q.E.D." is written at the end of a theorem; it means, "Quod erat demonstrandum"—"Which was the point to be demonstrated," to translate freely. In other words, each theorem begins with a prospective judgment. But that statement of the theorem is in effect a question for reflection: Is this theorem really true? The process pursued in the body of the theorem consists in logical proof. It may appeal to previously proved theorems, initial axioms, or constructions. Step by step one is brought from the starting point to the conclusion, which is the theorem originally considered: Q.E.D.

Logic is in fact a formalization of the process of grounding a judgment. Take the old standby: All men are mortal; Socrates is a man; therefore Socrates is mortal. The prospective judgment is "Socrates is mortal." The evidence is supplied in the two premises. The major premise is a general statement about a set of units called "men," who invariably have the characteristic "mortal." The second premise is to the effect that Socrates is a particular unit of the type referred to generally in the major premise. The conclusion then necessarily follows: Socrates has the characteristic of being mortal.

Logic isolates and renders explicit the grounding of a prospective judgment. In many ways it is a simplification, and may even seem a trivialization—common-sense judgments are often immensely more complicated. Questions could arise even as to how one would be absolutely sure that all men are mortal, or even whether Socrates is a man. But the process of logic isolates one step, saying, in effect, *if* it is true that all men are mortal, and *if* it is true that Socrates is a man, and if "men" and "man" are being used in the same sense—"men" referring to the general concept, of which "man" supplies a particular instance—*then* one certainly has the grounds to affirm that Socrates is mortal; or, to put it another way, the conclusion results necessarily from the premises.

If a single example may appear trivial, a sequence of logical steps, with the conclusions of one syllogism providing the premises for further syllogisms, can constitute a very powerful tool. It is also a product of the Greek enlightenment: the beginnings of it are found in Socrates leading his interlocutors by insistent questions through a series of logical steps to conclusions that sometimes disconcert them, or even contradict what they had said before. A certain maturity is found already in Aristotle, who codifies all the possible kinds of syllogisms, and the conditions under which their conclusions follow necessarily from their premises. But the idea had already been pioneered in a particular field by Euclid, who showed how a technique of following simple, logical steps could result in a whole body of geometric theorems. His achievement continues to attract admiration even in the modern period. Watson, it will be remembered, spoke of Holmes's science of deduction as aspiring to be "as infallible as propositions of Euclid." More impressively, Immanuel Kant, a proponent of the modern Enlightenment, at the beginning of the *Critique of Pure Reason,* his attempt to place philosophy on a fully scientific basis, harks back to this earlier model: "In the earliest times to which the history of human reason extends, mathematics, among that wonderful people, the Greeks, had already ventured upon the sure path of science" (trans. Norman Kemp Smith [London: MacMillan and Co., 1963] 19).

Justifying a Common-Sense Judgment

What precisely is a "sufficiency of evidence"? Geometry and logic have received special attention because they are special cases in which one can rely simply on logical necessity. If the rules of logic are followed, then the conclusion follows necessarily from the premises. But common-sense judgments are not so formalized. In a single day a person may make many judgments. If one were to try to put each of those judgments in syllogistic form, validate the logical process, and then ground the premises, it would undoubtedly require many more days to accomplish. So one returns to the question: When is the evidence sufficient for making a prospective judgment? Perhaps not surprisingly, there is no simple, logical answer to that question; rather a series of partial answers must be given.

The metaphor of a fortress is useful; the enemy to be defended against is error. The outer perimeter of the fort is a fence consisting of further questions *(see Figure 1).* Insights often give rise to further questions, and the same is true of the reflective insight. If the reflective insight, grasping the sufficiency of evidence for a prospective judgment, is followed by no further questions, this is a first indication of the sufficiency of evidence for a judgment.

Still, one may persist, how does one know there are no further questions? May it be that there *are* further questions, but I am simply ignorant of them?

The next and sturdier wall within the outside perimeter is called the self-correcting process of learning *(see Figure 2).* It has already been noted that later insights may modify and refine earlier ones; it has also been seen—dramatically, in the example of falling indecorously on ice-skates— how learning comes through mistakes as well as positive teaching. The learned person, then, is in a better position than the unlearned to be sure that there are no further questions concerning a reflective insight.

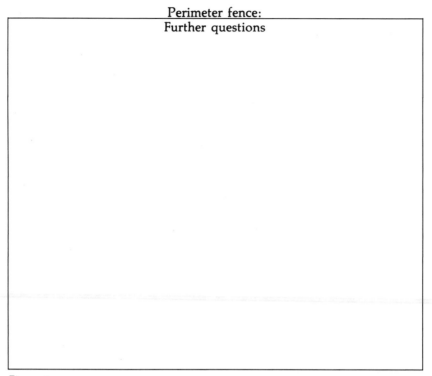

Figure 1

But there is a further aspect of the self-correcting process of learning: it concerns limited areas of the world of experience. Therefore, the issue is not whether there are *any* further questions—they are an unlimited multitude—but whether there are any further questions bearing on the point at hand, questions whose answers might materially affect the outcome of the reflective process. In short, the issue is whether there are any further *relevant* questions.

As that may be rather abstract, a simple example may be given. Suppose a man takes his car to a mechanic to be repaired. In the course of the initial dialogue, the man asks, "Just how much do you know about cabbages?" The mechanic might well be nonplussed. His customer has asked a further question; but the mechanic fails to see how it is a further *relevant* question. Knowing about cabbages might be expected of a farmer; it could be of help to a weekend gardener. The mechanic might fairly exclaim, "That has nothing to do with fixing cars!"

The mechanic may be an expert, say, on Chevrolet cars. He has perhaps studied them in trade school, in both theoretical and practical ways.

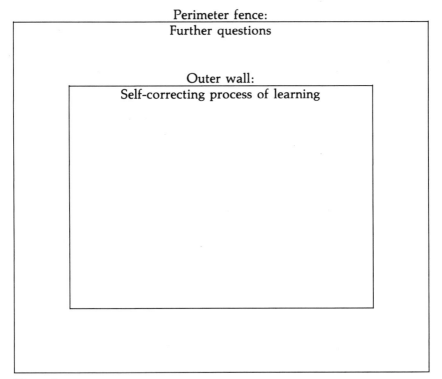

Figure 2

Further, he has a wealth of experience in repairing these cars; he has learned well from both his successes and his mistakes. Even if a particularly difficult case is given to him, he knows quickly how to isolate the problem, or to look up what he does not remember exactly. Such a person has become a master mechanic for a particular make of car. He is in the best position to say, there are no further relevant questions to be answered before making this judgment.

When the mechanic started learning, he probably didn't even know what the relevant questions were. As his store of insights gradually expanded, so did his questions. But in time those further questions received answers. The number of unanswered questions has diminished. The knower has mastered one area of knowing.

As it is a great advantage to the process of learning that we experience the world in large units, which repeat themselves, with identical or similar characteristics, so it is of great help to the knower that the universe divides into areas which can be mastered piecemeal. If it were necessary

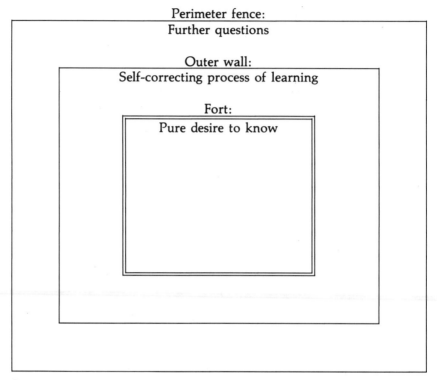

Perimeter fence:
Further questions

Outer wall:
Self-correcting process of learning

Fort:
Pure desire to know

Figure 3

to answer every question, relevant or irrelevant, before making a judgment, no judgments could be made at all. As it is, persons become specialists in one area of knowing, in a human division of labor. So one goes to a mechanic rather than an accountant to have his car repaired. An amusing aspect of that specialization can be found in Sherlock Holmes. He has an extensive and detailed knowledge of the annals of crime; but Watson is amazed to discover that Holmes does not know that the earth circles the sun. Futhermore, Holmes, once informed, assures Watson that he will promptly forget the fact, because he doesn't want to clutter his mind with useless information.

The person who has pursued the self-correcting process to its term in a certain area, then, is the proper person to pronounce on whether a reflective insight raises further questions. But note: this is true only in that area. If the mechanic, for example, decides to plant a weekend garden, then he may have to start from scratch to learn about cabbages, and pursue the whole curve of learning all over again. In the meantime, he should be cautious in making judgments outside his own area of expertise. Shoemaker, stick to your last!—because that is the area you know.

The journey to the center of the fort is also a journey "within"; not surprisingly then, the fort itself is constructed of a more personal reality, intellectual curiosity *(see Figure 3)*. To avoid erroneous judgments requires an openness of mind, an eagerness for further learning; in short, a readiness to greet further, relevant questions. Such an intellectual attitude may be absent for various reasons. It may be Friday night, for example, and the mechanic is anxious to finish his work. Rather than explore the car's problem fully, he just assumes the simplest possibility and effects an appropriate repair, hoping for the best. The castle, then, must have well-built walls of intellectual curiosity if it is not to let error slip through.

The next consideration is still more subjective. It is well known that some people are rash, ever tending to make judgments before the evidence is properly assembled. "You're always jumping to conclusions!" is a familiar complaint. On the other hand, other persons are Hamlet-like: they constantly find reasons to postpone making a judgment. A politician is

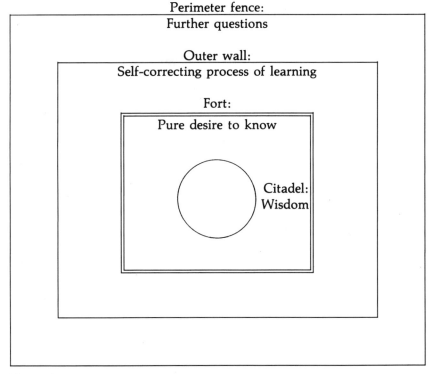

Figure 4

supposed to have said, "I won't say yes; and I won't say no; and I hesitate to say maybe." The one person rides rough-shod over any further relevant questions; the other is never satisfied that there might not be one further relevant question still to be discovered.

The citadel of the fortress, then, is a certain wisdom about weighing the evidence for judgment *(see Figure 4)*. That wisdom is aware of its own propensities toward either rashness or indecision, and tries to compensate for either. It is the fruit of long years of experience, of pursuing the mastery of perhaps many fields. It is the product of a constant openness to further questions. Toward gaining such wisdom guidelines and hints can be supplied; but it can be summarized in no simple set of logical rules.

Conclusion

The above analysis of the proper grounds of judgment not only reflects one aspect of cognitional process, it implies an intellectual morality: Never make a judgment that outruns the evidence.

In the structure being assembled, the question for reflection, the reflective insight, and the judgment round off the level of reflection:

	Judgment
Level of Reflection	Reflective insight
	Question for Reflection
	Concept
Level of Understanding	Insight
	Question for Understanding

16

Experience

The "materials of insight" have been mentioned already, but their discussion postponed; reference has also been made, almost unavoidably, to "experience," and even "the world of experience." But now the moment has come, in the inner journey, to visit explicitly the activity of experience.

Experience is such a basic word that it is hard to think of anything more common in terms of which to define it. It will be better to give some examples, the first of which will be sense experience. We have already mentioned how sense experience can have a metaphorical meaning—"insight"—but, prior to that, it has a literal meaning, which is the object here. I see a robin. Seeing is perhaps the most obvious and prized of the senses, but there are, as traditionally formulated, four others: hearing, feeling, tasting, and smelling. I hear the song of the robin; I smell the honeysuckle; I feel the warmth of the spring air; I taste the outdoor barbecue. Such experiences are almost too common to be remarked; yet they constitute our first and most rudimentary contacts with a world to be known.

The senses are easy enough to experiment with. Close the eyes, cover them with the hand, and one no longer sees; stop the ears, and one ceases to hear. A stuffy nose can prevent the sense of smell, an illness may make everything taste "off," and a local anesthetic deprives one part of the body of feeling. Sleep is the cessation of, or, at least, a selective inattention to, most sensory experience. In recent years, "sensory deprivation chambers" have been constructed, in which a person is perfectly suspended in water of body temperature, and sources of light, sound, and smell are totally closed out.

Traditionally one speaks of five senses, but there is at least a sixth: the kinesthetic. It is the sense of movement within the body. Touch is usually thought of as located in the skin; the kinesthetic sense registers the interior movement of the muscles. A kinesthetic sense is crucial, for example, in perfecting a golf swing or a tennis serve. The sense of balance in the inner ear is a seventh, and there may be others.

But besides direct sense experience, there is also sense memory, which is often constituted by images, in what is called the imagination. I may have seen the robin last spring; but now, in the dead of winter, with snow all around, I can still picture it exactly on the lawn. Similarly, there are auditory images; I can remember precisely how the robin sang. I may also be able to imagine the feel of the spring air, the smell of the honeysuckle, or the taste of the barbecue.

Some experimentation can also be done here by comparing notes. Some people may have technicolor images, and others black and white ones. For some people auditory imagination is much stronger than visual. A musician, for example, may be able to imagine from a score, without even humming, how the music would sound. There are also people who have no visual images, at least in their waking hours, but have rather a kinesthetic imagination.

Somewhere between a visual presentation and a visual image are diagrams. Examples would be the geometrical figures that Euclid used, or the diagrams of the benzene ring given above. They are seen by the eyes, and so in that way are visual presentations. But they are not pictures of reality, and so in that way are more like mental images.

Imagination represents a certain freedom in relation to sense experience. One may imagine what one has never seen: combining the wings of a great bird and a human figure, one may imagine an angel. Science itself, it may be noted, is growing in this direction of increasing freedom. Atoms and molecules have never been seen; they can only be imagined. But modern physics has conceived realities that cannot even be imagined. A photon is a "wavicle," something like a wave, and something like a particle; but it can only be adequately characterized in mathematical formulas. The mathematical notation, then, can be thought of as a highly abstract level of the diagram, but one where even a structural resemblance disappears; only a reference to mathematical relationships remains.

To this point the focus has been on the "outer" experience of the senses, either directly or in its transposition into imagination, as either memory or free construction. But there is also an "inner" experience, an awareness of mental activity. One can be aware of understanding as well as of seeing; of searching for an answer as well as listening intensely; of making a judgment as well as smelling a rose. The aim of much of the preceding pages has not been to create that experience—it is already widely given in common-sense experience, as ordinary language attests—but to heighten awareness of it, to examine it closely, to catalog and order it. If this effort has been successful, "inner" experience should now be almost as familiar as "outer" experience.

Again, there would seem to be an imaginational transposition of inner experience. Not only can I have an insight, I can also remember having it. Indeed, reflecting on an insight would almost necessitate holding it, somehow, in memory: how could I be reflecting on the insight if I have not yet had it? That memory may be carried by an image: I can picture Galileo in the cathedral of Pisa with the swinging lamp, or Newton in the orchard with the apple falling, not to recreate a visual image—I never actually saw these scenes—but to recapture the insight they had. The memory of an insight may be associated with a diagram which I can picture, or perhaps the kinesthetic memory of a geometrical construction. I may even be able to re-experience an insight merely by calling up the sense of excitement that originally accompanied it. (Question for further thought: what kind of sense is the "sense of excitement"?)

Experience, then, has been divided in two ways: as "inner" and "outer," and as direct and indirect, or imaginational. (The diagram is something between "inner" and "outer"; it may perhaps be thought of as an inner image which is re-expressed outwardly, visually.) The result is a fourfold division: an outer, direct (or sense) experience; its transposition into imaginal form; an "inner" experience of mental activity; and its transposition into imaginal form.

All of these are the raw materials of insight. An insight may be triggered by a direct sense experience, by an image of sense experience, or by a diagram; again, one may understand an inner experience, or the image of a mental activity. Finally, the outlines of mental activities that have been presented at the ends of all the recent chapters may be thought of as diagrams of inner experience; hopefully they too have sparked insight.

Some further questions about the interrelationships of these aspects of experience may be helpful. Can there be an insight merely into an image, without a direct sense or "inner" experience? It would seem so; a person may recall a visual presentation, or a diagram—or even a smell or a taste—and understand something not grasped originally (with the diagram, in fact, there may be no prior sense experience). Again, the reader may have, in the chapters on insight, remembered some past insight and understood more about it now than then.

Can there be, on the other hand, an insight into a direct experience, without an image? Or does the imagination always form some image to correspond to the direct sense experience? That is a finer point of mental activity which may be left for further introspective analysis.

With the distinction between sense and "inner" experience explicitated, it is now possible to say more precisely what has been evoked by the metaphor of an "inner journey." That journey, it can now be seen, has been an investigation of inner experience. As there can be study of outer experience, as in the physical sciences, so can there also be an examination of inner experience.

The myth of the cave may also be recurred to here. One possible reading is that Socrates is speaking of an ascent from outer, or sense, experience, into the realm of inner experience. It is in that inner experience, and not in sense experience (the world of shadows), that the knower will apprehend the true reality of things.

Finally, the explicit distinction of inner from outer experience allows a definition of "consciousness." Consciousness is precisely the realm of inner experience, within which the various cognitional activities take place.

More fully, consciousness is an awareness of an object, an act, and the self. "I see the robin" was the first and simplest example given of experience. The experience is, obviously and primarily, an awareness of the robin. But it is also an awareness of the "seeing." It is not that I see the robin unconsciously, and that I become conscious when I start to think about the "seeing"; I am already dimly conscious of the act of seeing. If not, I would be reflecting on an unconscious seeing of the robin. But if I am unconscious, I do not see the robin. I do not create, I only heighten that residual awareness by focusing on it.

Once more, I am also dimly aware of the "I." It is not that I am aware of the robin, and only become conscious of the I when I ask, who is seeing the robin? I am already conscious of the I. If not, I would be reflecting on an unconscious person seeing the robin; and an unconscious person does not see a robin. I do not create, I only heighten my self-awareness by reflecting explicitly on it.

To sum it up: I am conscious in both outer and inner experience. Consciousness is simply a characteristic of cognitional activity. It is the inner awareness of self, act, and object within any cognitional activity, either outer or inner.

Experience, then, adds to the foregoing account a prior level of presentations. It may be diagrammed as follows:

	Judgment
Level of Reflection	Reflective insight
	Question for Reflection

	Concept
Level of Understanding	Insight
	Question for Understanding

Level of Presentations	Image Outer Exper. (Sense)	Image Inner Exper. (Consciousness)

17

Retrospect and Implications

The full complement of mental activities has now been assembled, and it will be timely once more to examine the road that has been traveled, and to examine the implications of this completed structure.

The first thing to note is that the activities identified within consciousness are not isolated, but are closely related one to another. If we were merely animals, we would have nothing more than sense experience. But for human beings sense experience may lead to questions: What is that? Why did that happen? Who did this? These questions for understanding may, in turn, lead to insights—sometimes after a long search for understanding. But insight may lead to concept: the universal grasped by the insight under particular conditions is expressed in general form by the concept. But insight and concept only raise the question of their adequacy: Is this so? Is that true? This, in turn, sets in train a weighing of the evidence. When that process has been successfully concluded, judgment follows.

If the earlier moments lead to the later ones, it is also true that the later depend on the earlier. A judgment not preceded by a careful weighing of the evidence is but a rash statement. There would be no weighing of the evidence, however, unless it was evoked by the question for reflection. That question, in turn, would having nothing to reflect upon unless preceded by concept and insight. Concept, in turn, because it states in universal form what is grasped under particular conditions by insight, obviously presumes an insight. Insight, in its turn, would not arise without the questions for understanding which initiate the heuristic search. But the questions, finally, would have nothing to ask about unless there were a prior level of presentations, constituted by the experience of sense or consciousness.

The three levels may be summed up in terms of their principal activities: experience, insight, and judgment. Again, the same mutual relationship appears. Experience may lead to insights, because of questions for understanding; and insights, through questions for reflection, lead to judgments. Judgments, however, would have nothing to pronounce on, were there not prior insights; insight, conversely, would have nothing to understand, were there no prior experience.

Some comments have already been made about the difference between common-sense and scientific modes of thought; but the assembly of the full structure allows a fuller account, which may at once illuminate scientific method and show how the threefold structure is verified there.

A scientific investigation always begins by gathering data. Often it will involve measurement; sometimes it will include a search of the scientific literature, to gather the results of previous research. This is the level of experience.

But data by itself is mute, an unassimilated mass. What is then necessary is understanding. The scientist searches for meaningful correlations in the data, plausible explanations for the measurements. The fruit of this step is an hypothesis: this is the level of insight.

But one does not end with an hypothesis. Naturally the question arises, How do I know if this is true? The crucial experiment attempts to answer this question. The scientist tries to think of a test that will give one result if the hypothesis is true, and another if it is false. If the hypothesis is disconfirmed, then the scientist must return to prior steps: gathering more data, finding new correlations, or both. But if the hypothesis is confirmed, the scientist is in a position to make a positive judgment, which leads to a scientific theory and, perhaps in time, a basic law of science.

Science, then, is a way of coming to know. Because it is more methodical and self-conscious than common sense, it has reflected on its own process. That may be summed up briefly: gather data, make hypotheses, verify by crucial experiments. Since science is but one of the ways of knowing, however, its structure corresponds to that of the mental activities being investigated:

Judgment	Verify by crucial experiment
Insight	Make hypotheses
Experience	Gather data

The threefold structure reveals the key role of judgment. Judgment puts an end to one particular line of inquiry; it caps one moment of cognitional process. In it, the knower takes a stand, affirming something to be the case, to be true.

A single judgment, however, is obviously not the whole of knowing. Why is it, precisely, that the human mind raises questions about sense (or inner) presentations, and so ventures onto the level of understanding? What is the compulsion that addresses to an insight and its formulation an imperious, Is it so? What is, finally, the dissatisfaction with any particular judgment that leads, often immediately, to new observations, new insights, new questions for reflection?

The structure of experience-insight-judgment given above is static. But the human cognitional process is dynamic. It is always in movement, in virtue of what Lonergan calls "the drive to know." We experience within ourselves a thirst for knowledge. It is the curiosity that bubbles forth in the incessant questions of young children, and the more disciplined questions of inquiring adults. It is the force that creates libraries and spawns newspapers. It is the wonder that Aristotle identified as the beginning of philosophy in his *Metaphysics*. The drive to know has an object which is not as tangible as food, nor as palpable as a sexual partner. Yet there is a hunger and an eros of the mind that is quite as real as the desire for food or sex. It is the wonder that made Thales gaze at the stars, the quest of Galileo in the cathedral of Pisa or of Newton in the orchard at Woolsthorpe; it is the obsession that kept Goodyear looking, for years, for a way to transform rubber. The drive to know, then, may be added to the structure of mental activities as the dynamism that brings it into being, moves it from stage to stage, and ever goes beyond any present achievement in its search for greater knowledge.

If judgment is a key moment in cognitional process, then so is the question for understanding. The senses we share with animals: cats see, and dogs hear. It is the question for understanding that first moves the process to the level of a fully human knowing. Earlier it was said that insight manifests a certain freedom in relation to its underlying materials. Now the reason for that can be seen: on the level of insight the prior deliverances of sense (or consciousness) are treated with a creative intelligence, which can fashion hypotheses, seek new correlations, envision in concept the formal universal; the senses are always limited to the particular.

We may suggest still another reading of Plato's many-faceted myth of the cave. Socrates is calling for a journey from the shadows and images of sense to the higher knowing of the human mind, where things are seen in their true light. That ascent is painful, for our sense apprehension of the world is familiar and comfortable, and a journey into the mind and its proper knowing is arduous. Yet it is a journey we must undertake, if we are to know ourselves.

We have located an intellectual morality in the responsibility of judgment, and the possibility of probable and even withheld judgments: if we

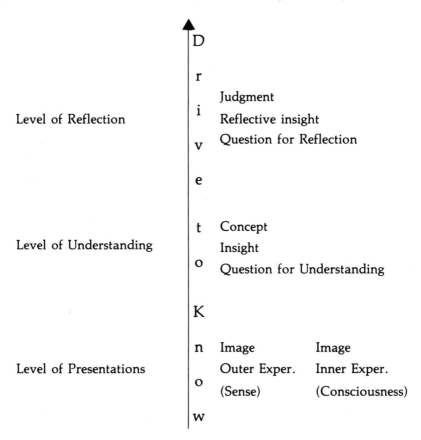

are to be true even to ourselves, to our internal drive to know, from insight to the question for reflection, through the weighing of evidence, to judgment, we must resolve never to make a judgment without possessing appropriate evidence. The expanded structure of knowing allows a wider statement of that intellectual morality. If knowing begins on the level of presentations, then the corresponding mandate is, Be attentive. "Look before you leap," is the way common sense puts it. "Keep your eyes peeled," "keep your ears open." Jesus was wont to say, "Let him who has ears to hear, hear." Both science and Holmes's science of deduction begin with observation, and Holmes may serve as a model of attentiveness.

But attentiveness without intelligence is just staring with the eyes, straining with the ears. As the level of insight supervenes on the level of presentations, so it implies a new mandate: Be intelligent. "Think!" as the father urges the boy doing homework. "Put brain in gear before engaging mouth!" as it is sometimes humorously expressed. A model of fidelity to the intellectual search may well be found in the great figures of science.

Even insights, however, are but a dime a dozen if they are not verified. As the level of understanding is followed by the level of reflection, so a third mandate emerges: Be judicious. Do not extend your conclusions beyond the available evidence. Perhaps the appropriate model here is Solomon, judge of fabled wisdom.

It may again be helpful to summarize this in a diagram:

Judgment	Be judicious
Insight	Be intelligent
Experience	Be attentive

18

The Boomerang Effect

The Australian aborigines craft a small object which, when thrown, returns to the place from which it originated. The reader may have noted in these pages a fascination with activities and realities that return upon themselves. Socrates turned words upon themselves to create definitions, as seen in chapter 9. Chapter 10 showed how an insight may grasp other insights, and also recalled the moment when mind became cognizant of itself in scientific method. The question was turned upon itself in chapter 11, and the psychologist was seen, in chapter 12, to study the psychologist. (Whether the snake biting its own tail belongs in this series could be debated!) To avoid more technical terms, this may be called the boomerang effect.

All of the mental activities singled out so far can also be turned back upon themselves, and it will be the burden of the present chapter to detail how that is so; forthcoming chapters will examine the implications of this peculiar characteristic of cognitional process.

Insight

Insight can be turned upon mental activities. It is possible to understand experience, for example, as the initiatory level of cognitional process. In chapter 16 it was seen how this is illustrated especially by sense experience. It was also seen how sense experience can be transposed into images, how experience also comprises the inner experience of consciousness (with its associated images), and that each of these experiences can occasion insight.

But if insight can understand experience, it can also grasp how the question for understanding moves the human knower from the status of passive observer to that of alert, inquiring intelligence. Not only that, but insight may grasp insight itself. The chapter on jokes showed how one insight may grasp other insights, but that was slightly different: the higher insight grasped and integrated the *contents* of the lower insights. But the claim here is that insight may also understand the *act* of insight. That was, in fact, the thrust of chapters 4–10, and, to the extent that they communicated successfully, the reader will have understood, through the examples given and possibly through personal experiences, what an insight is. Conception, too, was offered for understanding as the formal and abstract generalization of the universal captured under particular conditions by the insight.

If insight can grasp the meaning of experience and insight, however, it can also understand how the question for reflection moves the cognitional process to a new level of verification or checking. That question, it was understood, led to a process called weighing the evidence; which terminated, it was finally understood, in the commitment of the judgment.

The previous chapter summarized the above and integrated it with the drive to know, thus offering the reader a synthetic insight into the operations of intelligence. Insight, therefore, can be turned back upon the whole cognitional process.

Question for Understanding

But what is true of insight is equally true of the question for understanding. For one may ask such questions as, What is experience? What are the senses? What is inner experience, or consciousness? What are images?

The question for understanding may be turned directly upon itself by asking, What is the question for understanding? Again, what is insight? What is the concept? What is the question for reflection? What is weighing the evidence? What, finally, is judgment?

Concept

Not only can one ask these questions and understand the answers, it is possible to formulate them conceptually in the abstract. Then one speaks of them, not in this or that particular instance, but as they are generally, in every case. Since the concept is closely linked with definition, it may be helpful here to offer definitions of all the mental activities recognized.

Experience is that mental activity which provides the initial materials for cognitional process.

Sense experience is that mental activity by which we first apprehend the world, through sight, hearing, smell, taste, and touch (and any related senses).

Consciousness is that mental activity by which we are aware of object, act, and self.

Imagining is that mental activity by which we re-present the apprehensions of sense or consciousness.

The question for understanding is that mental activity which addresses the experience of sense or consciousness, or an image, and moves cognitional process toward fully human knowing.

The insight is that mental activity which grasps a pattern in the previously disorganized data of sense, consciousness, or imagination.

Conception is that mental activity which formulates the universal, grasped by insight under particular conditions, in an explicit and abstract way.

The question for reflection is that mental activity which addresses insight and concept with an, Is it so? Is it true?

Weighing the evidence is that mental activity which assesses the sufficiency of evidence for a prospective judgment.

Judgment is that mental activity which ends one moment of cognitional process, and in which the knower takes a stand by asserting something to be the case.

Experience

If it is possible to understand cognitional process, that is, of course, only because it can first be experienced. One may experience sensing in a heightened way, for example, by opening and closing one's eyes. The experience of the question for intelligence becomes prominent when one is in the throes of trying to understand a difficult problem; and insight is experienced as the breakthrough that offers an answer to that question, and releases the tension. The concept becomes explicit matter of experience when one tries to formulate a definition, saying in an abstract and universal way what was grasped in insight. The experience of the question for reflection can be like throwing cold water on a bright idea, as it searchingly asks, Is that so? Weighing the evidence is experienced as the sifting of pros and cons, while judgment itself is experienced as responsible assertion. That is perhaps no more true than when one is charged with being wrong.

Whether a person experiences experience, or is aware of awareness, however, is a nice question; it will be left for more subtle introspective investigations.

Question for Reflection

The operations of experience and understanding, then, can be turned back upon cognitional process itself. But the same is true for the operations on the level of reflection. So the person may ask, Is it true that the human knower experiences? has sense experience? is interiorly aware of his or her mental activities? represents those experiences by faithful and even creative imagination? Is it the case that one inquires of these presentations, what, why, who, when, where, how? or with the mathematicians, What is x? or with the scientist, What is the nature of . . .? Is it really true that a person understands, grasps patterns by insights, expresses them formally in the general concept? Is it really the case that one inquires, Is it really the case . . .? that one weighs the evidence for and against a proposition? that persons, finally, commit themselves by a definitive or, less substantially, by a probable judgment?

Weighing the Evidence

If one may ask the question, one may also weigh the evidence. What evidence, in fact, is there for experience? sensing? imagining? the awareness of consciousness? the question for understanding? the insight? the concept? the question for reflection? the weighing of evidence? the judgment?

Judgment

And finally, a person may entertain a judgment about all these matters. If the evidence is sufficient, one might affirm experience, sensing, imagining, the inner awareness of consciousness. A person might assert that there exists a question for understanding, an insight which responds to it, a concept which formulates it abstractly. One might commit oneself to the proposition that there truly is such a thing as the question for reflection, the weighing of the evidence, and the consequent judgment.

Drive to Know

Before closing, it may be noted that the same process may be applied to the drive to know. A person can experience the drive to know as a compelling curiosity that rouses one from the lethargy of sense reverie to the stern task of understanding, that also applies to that understanding the imperious test of reflection, and then moves one from any particular judgment to further experiences, further questions, further insights. Can the drive to know be applied to itself? Perhaps it already has. It is the curiosity that led the author to study Lonergan's treatise on knowing; and it is undoubtedly the interest that has sustained the reader in pursuing the project to this point.

In brief summary, all the operations of cognitional process can be turned—in what has been called the boomerang effect—upon themselves. That process heads, in the last analysis, to a judgment affirming the structure of knowing as it has been assembled.

19

The Affirmation of Cognitive Process

A judgment has been envisioned; but now the moment in the inner journey has come to turn from hypothetical proposal to commitment. As already seen, however, there is an intellectual morality that governs judgment; and so the judgment must be preceded by a critical review of the evidence.

From the start, it has been stressed that the inner journey into consciousness is also a personal one; to underline that aspect, this chapter will be written as a series of questions, addressed in the second person from the author to the reader. An answer to the questions will be provided by a hypothetical reader, but it is up to the individual reader to substitute his or her own answers to the questions.

Do you enjoy sense experience?

That's an easy one. Of course! I am not blind; I see. I am not deaf, so I hear. I touch with my hands and feel impressions on my skin. I may not be as good at smelling as some of the people around me, but I can detect odors, at least if I'm not suffering from hay fever. Yes, I can taste as well. I'm not quite sure if I understand this kinesthetic sense, but I can tell when my golf swing has been a good one; and I have a reasonably good sense of balance.

Can you make a judgment, then, that you experience through the senses?

Yes, I can. In fact, as I understand it, that is what I just did—I made judgments about each of the senses. Unless you have something more subtle in mind?

No, that's all I meant. If you understood the question, then the sufficient evidence is supplied merely by having the experience of sensing. Now, do you experience imagining?

Yes, I certainly experience images. They are more often black and white than color. I can easily picture for myself a diagram, as for a problem in geometry. Sometimes I like to use stick figures for people. But I wouldn't make a very good artist; I don't imagine in enough detail.

Have you been able to experience your own mental activities?

Yes, I've managed that fairly well. I guess I was always aware of them, but I must admit that what I've read here has called them much more to my attention. I think insight is the easiest to recognize; not only could I follow most of the examples—some of the scientific ones were difficult— but I've been noticing it especially when I do crossword puzzles. I'll need a word, and sometimes it will come immediately, but other times I'll really have to cast around for it. I remember one morning when I woke up with the word I couldn't for the life of me think of the day before.

And do you experience images of those mental activities?

That's a little harder. I guess I must do something like that, because I just recalled an insight. So I must have some way of bringing it back to mind. But how exactly I do that I find hard to specify. Am I remembering the feel of the sheets as I woke up that morning? Or does the crossword puzzle pop back into mind as a set of black and white squares? Do I remember the clue to the word? Or did I wake up mumbling the word? That was just a little while ago, and already I'm not quite sure. Maybe it was all of them together.

Do you ask questions?

Of course I do—that goes without saying! How else would I get information from people? But I've been thinking about the idea that the question for understanding really does start a whole new level of knowing. I'm beginning to think that's true. The other day some friends and I were talking about Nathaniel Hawthorne's *The Scarlet Letter*—we're studying it in American Literature. And someone asked, "When did he live?" We weren't sure whether it was the seventeenth or eighteenth century. One of my friends said, "Who cares?" But for some reason it bugged me. I wanted to know. So I looked it up—1804–64. Somehow, I think that fact's going to stick in my mind. And that gave me a further insight: as I thought back over my education, it came to me that the things I remember best are the ones that have become personal questions.

Do you ever have insights?

Thanks a lot! Do you think I'm stupid? Of course I understand things. Sometimes, naturally, it takes longer than other times. To be truthful, I'm not a genius. My older brother always seems to catch on faster than I do. It's not just that he's older, either—he's always been that way. Still, I'm not a dummy. I get mostly Bs in school, some As; and I'm sure I could do better if I really wanted to work at it.

Do you have concepts?

I'm having a harder time here. If you want to know whether I recognize general things, the answer is yes. I can tell a telephone pole from a crocodile, a piece of granite from a hibiscus as well as the next guy. I know what a definition is too, and I even think I can be fairly good at making one up—maybe it's all the time with the crosswords. But when I try to put my finger on exactly how or when I come to those general concepts, then, I must admit, it gets pretty murky. I'll keep working on that one.

Do you ask questions for reflection?

Yes, I do. You can't just say the first thing that comes to your mind; you should pause a bit, count to ten, and ask, Is that really true? And I have a good example. The other day my older sister's husband came home; he's always on to some loopy idea or other. This time he was saying that all the music in the world was based on just three melodies; everything else was only variation. Well, I challenged him right away: "Where do you get these wacko theories?" I added sarcastically, "Sure, I suppose there's the kind of song that starts low and goes high, and the one that starts high and ends low, and the one that ends up about where it began." "What kind of proof," I concluded, "can you offer for this off-the-wall idea?" Naturally, he didn't have any answer.

Do you have experience of weighing the evidence for a judgment?

Yes, and I'm becoming more careful about that. I never thought much about it before, but the caution about not making a judgment without sufficient evidence really brought me up short. I'm getting better, but I still talk too quickly, like I know it all. I got into a problem with that the other day at work. I sounded absolutely positive about something—and it turned out I was wrong! When I thought about it later, I realized there are some things I know a lot about, and others I'm not so familiar with. I notice it's in the areas I'm not so up on that I make my mistakes.

Do you make judgments?

Of course—I do that all the time! Next question?

Do you experience the drive to know?

You sort of snuck that one in at the end, didn't you—and I haven't had as much time to think about it! But if you're asking whether I'm ever curious, yes, I am—like the other day, when I just had to know Hawthorne's dates. And if you're asking whether I like to get my facts straight, and be correct in what I'm saying, yes I do. Whether the drive to know is always leading me into new questions—well, there, to be honest, it varies. Sometimes I really enjoy learning new things, and I can get all excited about it. Other times, yes, I'd like to know ever so much, but it just seems like so much work!

Well, then, are you ready to affirm the whole structure of the cognitional process? I'll repeat the diagram as a review.

```
                              ▲
                              │ D
                              │
                              │ r
                              │     Judgment
                              │ i
   Level of Reflection        │     Reflective insight
                              │ v
                              │     Question for Reflection
                              │
                              │ e
                              │
                              │
                              │ t   Concept
   Level of Understanding     │     Insight
                              │ o
                              │     Question for Understanding
                              │
                              │
                              │ K
                              │
                              │ n   Image              Image
   Level of Presentations     │     Outer Exper.       Inner Exper.
                              │ o
                              │     (Sense)            (Consciousness)
                              │
                              │ w
                              │
```

Whoa—just a minute! What exactly am I letting myself in for here? I realize I have pretty much said yes to all of these mental activities in isolation. But what is added when they are all put together? Am I also affirming the order in which they occur? Of course, some parts of that appear pretty clear too. A question for reflection has to have something to reflect on, so the level of understanding has to come first. And there wouldn't be much to understand without some kind of experience. But does knowing always follow exactly this order? Is it possible that someone might have just asked a question for reflection, when a new experience crashes in upon him, calling for a revised understanding? Or might not someone be trying to make a definition, and realize he really doesn't understand after all?

I also wonder, is this schema complete? I may have good evidence to affirm all these activities; but maybe there are others. I can't think of any at the moment, but that doesn't mean they don't exist. It's really fairly recently I've started studying this; I suppose you could literally spend years examining your own consciousness.

And here's a further point: This is Lonergan's account of knowing. I suppose other philosophers must have tried to do the same thing. Maybe I should study all of them before I commit myself.

Now, however, I may be overreacting. I could be like the politician who hesitated to say maybe. So let me make a carefully limited statement, as I've been learning to do: Aside from some fuzzy areas, and barring future contrary information, I affirm this structure of knowing, as far as it goes, to be highly probable, and to match what I've observed of my own consciousness.

Conclusion

The judgment affirming the structure of mental activities is, in many ways, the high point of the journey being pursued here. Up to it everything to this point has been leading; and a largely positive answer to the questions, and a substantial affirmation of the structure presented, will be the premise of the remaining chapters.

20

Cognitional Structure as Self-Justifying

The envoi of the last chapter may have seemed rather abrupt. A positive answer to the questions was presumed for the rest of the journey. But suppose there were readers who could not, in good intellectual conscience, answer yes to those questions. Aren't they being dumped rather unceremoniously at this point? The author would not want to be ungracious to a heretofore loyal reader, so this question deserves an answer before we move on to the main matter of this chapter.

Suppose someone answered no to the first question. That person would never have had any sense experience, as if raised from birth in a sensory-deprivation chamber. But then, it may be pointed out, the person would never have seen a book, and so could never have read up to this point. So there need be no concern for such a "reader."

Suppose, less drastically, that a person is blind. But that person would not have to deny all sense experience, only the experience of sight. No doubt the person will have read the text to this point in a Braille edition, or by having someone read the book out loud. The rest of the text could be pursued in the same way. Concern for this hypothetical reader is unnecessary.

Perhaps there is a reader who experiences sense consciousness, but has no awareness of the data of consciousness. Such a person could hardly answer yes to that question, and would have to drop out of the pursuit at this point. But, by the definition given already, a person unaware of self, object, and act is unconscious. Unconscious persons do not read, so again a worry about such a hypothetical reader is misplaced.

Suppose someone were to say, I recognize the experience of sense and of consciousness, but I've never had an insight, so I had to answer no to that question. Were there such a reader, all the previous chapters would have been mere marks on paper, as though someone paged through a book in a totally foreign language. It would seem purely accidental, then, that such a person would give up at this point rather than another. Besides, this person would never have understood what a book was for, and so would probably not be looking at it in the first place. Concern about such a hypothetical reader would appear to be far-fetched.

Let us suppose the reader says, I accept experience and insight, but have never made a judgment, so must answer no to that question. But such a person would not have been in a position to judge that this was the place to put down the book, or even to judge that reading the book was a worthwhile expenditure of time in the first place. Worry about such a hypothetical reader seems, again, misplaced.

Suppose, more plausibly, that a person would answer, I recognize some of those experiences, but not others; I am also aware of some you did not mention. Therefore, I cannot, in good intellectual conscience, say yes to the schema you proposed. Quite so. But then the hypothetical reader will be seen to have discovered personally precisely those activities of experiencing, understanding, weighing the evidence, and making the corresponding judgment which have been proposed.

Or suppose that a hypothetical reader answers, I recognize in myself exactly those activities you mention, but I organize them in quite a different way in my own mind; I must disagree with your judgment, and put forward my own. But then, again, the reader has discovered personally precisely those activities of experience, understanding, and judging for a sufficient reason which the schema comprises.

Perhaps the various suppositions may allay any fears about readers who have to be left behind at this point.

The fact is, the affirmations that have been made in the last chapter are very peculiar ones, because of the characteristic of mental activities that they can be turned back upon themselves. They are not exactly self-evident propositions, in the sense that, once one understands the meaning of the terms, one has to affirm the proposition (e.g., the whole is greater than the part). But they are, one may say, "self-protected propositions," in the sense that affirming their opposites is incoherent. It is this self-justifying aspect which must now be examined.

It may be seen most easily with judgment. It is incoherent to make a judgment, There is no judgment. This is not exactly a logical contradiction. A logical contradiction exists when two propositions are diametrically opposed (e.g., judgment exists, and judgment does not exist). In this case, there is only one proposition, There is no judgment. That proposition stands in tension, not with another proposition, but with the mental activity of affirming it, the very act of judging. So to judge, Judgment exists, is a coherent activity, because the very activity itself provides the sufficient evidence for making the judgment. Whereas to judge, There is no judgment, is an incoherent activity, because the very act of judging provides evidence to upset the judgment simultaneously being made. It is as if one were taking away with the left hand what one was positing with the right hand. Note that this does not apply to all judgments, but only to those where the mental activity is being turned upon itself, where the act of judging concerns judgment. Thus, it may be perfectly coherent to judge, This is a five-pound sack of potatoes, or, this is not a five-pound sack of potatoes, depending on the facts of the case. But when the very content of the judgment concerns the existence of judgment, it is coherent to judge, Judgment exists, but incoherent to judge, Judgment does not exist. The affirmation of judgment is self-justifying, then, in that its alternative is incoherent.

In a similar way, it is coherent to ask, Is there a question for reflection? But to answer the question there is no need for further information, because the very posing of the question constitutes the sufficient evidence for a yes. Conversely, a no would be incoherent. For if there were no question for reflection, then the question could never have been asked in the first place.

Again, one may coherently weigh the evidence to determine whether there is a weighing of evidence. What one cannot coherently do is to end that process by assessing that there is no weighing of the evidence. For weighing the evidence is itself sufficient evidence for the assertion that there is a weighing of the evidence. Were there no weighing of the evidence, the person would not have been weighing the evidence in the first place.

A person may coherently conceive of a universe in which there is no conception. What one cannot coherently do is to conceive *this* universe as having no conception, because the very act of conceiving this universe as having no conception would constitute at least one exception. Were there no conception, one would not be conceiving another universe, or this universe, in the first place.

Again, it would be incoherent to have an insight that there is no such thing as insight. Were there no insight, one would understand neither the presence nor the absence of understanding.

Once more, it is coherent to ask, What is a question? But the very act of asking the question not only establishes the existence of the question, but reveals, in an example, something of its nature. So the scientist might pursue the matter, quite coherently, by asking, What is the nature of the question? What would be incoherent here would be to deny that the question exists, or that it has no nature or determinate form. To question the question, not in the sense of inquiring about it, but in the sense of undermining its existence or determinate nature, is an incoherent activity, because one establishes by the very asking what one would undermine or eliminate.

Above it was left undetermined whether there is any meaning to "experiencing experience," or "being aware of awareness." Without making any determination on that, the application in this case may be made hypothetically: If there is such a thing, experiencing experience would be a coherent activity, whereas experiencing a total lack of experience would be incoherent. Again, being aware of awareness could be coherent; but being aware of a total lack of awareness would be incoherent.

Finally, the drive to know could coherently be a drive to know the drive to know. One may wonder what wonder is; but one could not coherently wonder whether wonder exists.

In summary, the affirmations sought and made in the last chapter are not just any assertions, but privileged judgments. Because of the possibility that mental activities can be turned back upon themselves, these affirmations are self-justifying, in the sense that attempting to deny them immediately involves the knower in an incoherence between the mental activity itself and its content.

21

A New Science

In the last chapter it was mentioned that a scientist might want to ask, What is the nature of the question? That suggests the possibility of approaching mental activities in a scientific way. It will be the purpose of this chapter to follow up that suggestion.

Chapter 4 showed how insight is already a part of common-sense awareness. Chapter 9 contrasted common-sense and scientific modes of understanding. The juxtaposition implies a parallel: as common-sense knowledge of the physical world gradually gave way to the scientific mode of the physical sciences, so it is possible that a common-sense grasp of mental activities may yield to a scientific approach to them.

As already noted, common-sense knowing has practical ends, while science values knowing as an end in itself. The same contrast would apply here: mental activities are not entirely unrecognized by common-sense awareness, but they are noticed only to the extent that they are valuable in getting practical things done. A science of mental activities would seek an ordering and understanding of cognitional process as a good in itself; naturally, its investigation would be more thorough and consistent than the attention afforded in passing to these activities in common-sense awareness.

Two general realms of meaning, then, have been recognized: common sense and science. The proposal here is to add a third: interior science. Both comparisons and contrasts may be noted with the physical sciences already studied.

The emergence of science in the Greek context, it was noted, required a prior development of common sense, as well as a certain leisure to allow learning for its own sake. For the emergence of the third stage of an interior science, probably both those prior developments are prerequisites.

Without a certain leisure and interest in knowledge for its own sake, probably no more attention would be given to mental activities than is commonly accorded them by common sense. But without a model to hand of the move from common sense to science, as illustrated with sensible phenomena in the Greek and the modern Enlightenments, it would be difficult to approach scientifically the more elusive phenomena of inner experience.

The Greek move to science, it was also noted, began with the Socratic quest for definition. That suggests a way to begin, by defining the mental activities in question. As it happens, that has already been accomplished in chapter 18; the reader may want to review those definitions if they have become hazy.

A further parallel may be noted between the physical sciences and the science of consciousness: they both begin in experience, and therefore with their proper data.

That introduces also, however, the principal contrast between the two sciences: the physical sciences are grounded in sense data, while inner science takes its stand upon the data of consciousness. Nevertheless, the proposal here is that there is an analogy between the two constructions.

This difference of starting point also leads to a deeper contrast between the two sciences. In the physical sciences, basic terms are constantly subject to revision. The concept of *mass* has already been remarked. It proved very useful in Newtonian science. But nothing ensures that it is absolutely necessary, and nothing precludes that a future revision of scientific theory might scrap it. Thus *space* and *time* were basic terms in Newtonian physics. But in Einstein's revision of scientific theory, they are seen to be derivative and secondary. The new constant is understood to be the speed of light. Rather than three dimensions of space, and a totally unrelated factor of time, there are now four dimensions, and under certain conditions of change from one reference frame to another, what is spatial in one frame may be partially transposed into the temporal in another. The point to be grasped is that basic terms in the physical sciences are matters of discovery, and new discoveries may always make old ones outdated. Basic terms come and go; only the method of the physical sciences remains constant.

The basic terms of the science of consciousness, however, will not be subject to revision. For they are the mental activities themselves, and, as seen in the last chapter, those activities are, in a certain sense, self-justifying. Trying to revise them would only land the prospective reviser in incoherence.

The science of consciousness, therefore, will have the advantage that its basic terms are not subject to revision. That does not mean the science is closed, or excludes further questions. In the journey already pursued, numerous further questions have been strewn along the path for deeper and more subtle introspective investigations. But the science of inner experience will enjoy a solid core that is unrevisable and stable.

That may appear a bold claim, and it requires some evidence to back it up. First, one must ask, what precisely is "revision"? Referring back to the parallel of the physical sciences, it would appear that revision could mean one of two things. On the one hand, it is the result of more accurate measurements. A good example here is Galileo and the pendulum. His first approximation was that the period of the pendulum required exactly the same amount of time, no matter how broad or narrow the path of the swings. But further measurements showed that this was not quite the case: there are in fact subtle differences of time, especially when there is a wide variation between swings.

On the other hand, revision can be the result of a new understanding of data already given. A good example here is in Kekule's work. The data he was working with were available to other scientists. His unique contribution was the insight that the data could be explained if the carbon atoms were arranged in a ring, with alternating single and double bonds around the ring.

Revision, then, can occur only if there appear new data, or if old data are given a new understanding. It can only take place by appeal to experience or insight. But one can hardly appeal to experience to revise the activity of experience; nor can one appeal to insight to revise the activity of insight.

To put it another way, a revision implies a new judgment, which states something to be the case which is at variance with the old judgment. Making such a judgment requires evidence; otherwise it will be unreasonable. But a judgment takes a stand on prior insights and experiences; and so a new judgment, as just seen, will require either new experience, or new insights, or both.

Revision, therefore, in its very meaning recapitulates the basic structure of knowing as experience, insight, and judgment. Therefore it would be altogether incoherent to propose a revision of this basic structure. The basic core of the new science of consciousness is necessarily unrevisable.

The reason, of course, that the basic terms of cognitional science are not revisable, while those of the natural sciences are, is that in the natural sciences the activities of the mind are turned upon the data of sense, offered by the physical world, while the mental activities, in the science of consciousness, return upon themselves. In the science being proposed, then, the mental activities are explicitly, deliberately, and systematically turned upon themselves, in contrast to the sporadic and partial attention they receive in common-sense awareness. Once those activities receive a basic formulation, such as was achieved in chapter 17, that formulation will function as a stable and unrevisable core grounding the future progress and expansion of the science.

To illuminate further the project being undertaken here, it may be helpful to compare it with a similar one. René Descartes was undoubtedly trying to found his philosophy upon such an unshakable foundation. He thought that he had found it in the *Cogito*. In one of the most famous sentences in all philosophy, he reasoned, "Cogito, ergo sum": "I think, therefore I am." He argued, even if I doubt, I am thinking, because doubting is a form of thinking; so even if I doubt whether I am thinking, I by that very activity establish my conclusion. Descartes, then, wanted to found his new science on the inner experience of thinking; the similarities with the present proposal are evident. From that stable basis he argued to the existence of God, and from there to the existence of the external world.

Some differences also emerge, however, when the present project is contrasted with Descartes's, and they will provide further insight into the meaning of the science of cognition.

In the first place, it may be noted, the present proposal is more modest than Descartes's. He apparently argued from thinking to existence, from "I think" to "I am." The science of cognition is not trying to argue to the existence of the self. In fact, Descartes's procedure, which appears so obvious and even persuasive when one is first acquainted with it, becomes difficult to pin down when one inquires into it more exactly; scholars dispute precisely what he was doing.

If Descartes's argument is taken as a strict demonstrative logic, then one notes that it is really not a syllogism—the "ergo" notwithstanding—but only a minor premise and a conclusion.

> I think.
> Therefore I am.

To make that a true syllogism, one would have to supply a major premise.

> Whatever thinks, exists.
> But I think.
> Therefore I exist.

The logic is now impeccable, but one must ask for the proof of the major premise. It is perhaps not so far-fetched. Medieval philosophy held to the principle "operatio sequitur esse": "operation follows being." Usually that was understood to mean that the kind of operations something performs flows from the kind of being it is. It is the same idea that politicians use in a common-sense way when they say, If it looks like a duck, walks like a duck, and quacks like a duck, then it must be a duck. But the medieval adage could also be understood in a deeper sense: nothing can operate unless it first exists. That would seem to buttress Descartes's absent major premise.

In fact, however, Descartes never undertakes to prove the major premise, and, at the beginning of his work, he rather ostentatiously sets aside the medieval tradition of philosophy. As an argument, then, his basic statement is lacking—though, again, scholars debate whether he really meant it as a demonstration.

Whatever Descartes's intentions, the present proposal is initially more modest. To put it in Cartesian terms, it might be worded, "Cogito, ergo cogito": "I think, therefore I think." That may appear so modest as to be a mere tautology, except that the "I think" is not the same in both cases. In the first instance it refers to an activity; in the second, to a judgment. The meaning therefore is, Because I engage in the activity of thinking, I can truly affirm that I think. Not only can I affirm that, but it is a privileged and a self-justifying judgment, because it would be incoherent to think that I don't think, or that I am not now thinking.

In another way, however, the present science of consciousness is more ambitious, because it attempts a full catalogue of mental activities as a foundation. Descartes's foundation is a rather undifferentiated "thinking," which he distinguishes from "doubting." (In terms of the structure already developed, "thinking" is probably best identified with the level of understanding, or understanding plus reflection, whereas "doubting" is that mental activity of hesitating whether to make a judgment, because the evidence does not seem to be forthcoming.) Elsewhere he does speak of sitting by a warm fire, and feeling the consistency of a piece of wax in his hands; as will be seen in another chapter, he also places much weight on the concept. Nevertheless, "thinking" is his basis, and he quickly moves on to prove the existence of God and the physical world. The science being attempted here, on the other hand, would investigate the cognitional operations thoroughly before proceeding further.

Another difference is that the present effort at a cognitional science lays less emphasis on proof than Descartes does. In particular, Descartes's procedure of proving the existence of God, then arguing that I have sensations, then that a good God could not have placed them in me to deceive me, so that an external world must exist, seems misguided. With good reason, that argument has persuaded few people. Here, sense experience and inner experience are equally given, equally data. Each in its own way is the starting point for knowing: the two together are the starting point of common-sense knowing; sense experience is the starting point of the natural sciences; and inner experience is the starting point of cognitional science. One cannot demonstrate such starting points, for the very attempt to do so will inevitably appeal to those starting points themselves. One does not demonstrate any of the mental activities, then, but discovers them; or perhaps better, one only calls more explicit attention to what has already been more casually discovered. The thought, in particular, that one could appeal to the more obscure (the inner experience) to ground the less obscure (sense experience) is therefore wrong-headed; and it remains the source of much that is most objectionable about Cartesianism.

Finally, the present effort does not accord to universal doubt the key importance Descartes ascribed to it. He proposed to begin by doubting everything: whatever would emerge from such a test would clearly be indubitable. That is why thinking became the key point of entry: even if one doubted thinking, that was indubitably a form of thinking. The fact is, however, that if one doubts everything, then one has no place to start at all. So Cardinal Newman sagely observed, if one were forced to choose between believing nothing and believing everything, it would be better to do the latter, for then there would be a hope of gradually eliminating one's mistaken beliefs.

In the end, then, Descartes puts too much stress on demonstration and proof. Demonstration works best with the universal and the necessary, with what has to be:

> All men are mortal.
> Socrates is a man.
> Therefore Socrates is mortal.

Compare:

> Some men have red hair.
> Descartes was a man.
> Therefore Descartes may or may not have had red hair.

The conclusion in both cases is true, but the second does not seem to be a very useful truth. Cognitional science does not demonstrate the necessary; like modern science, it merely seeks to grasp what in fact is so. I do not have to exist; it just happens that I do. There is no absolute necessity that I engage in mental activities; in fact I experience myself doing so. Perhaps those mental activities could have been other than they are; but in fact they are not. The proper method of interior science, then, is not demonstration, but discovery: the experience, the understanding, and the judgment as to what my mental activities in fact are. But once those activities are called to attention, understood, and organized in this more modest way, one has nevertheless an indubitable basis for the further pursuit of the science of consciousness.

22

Further Reflection on Cognitional Process

A science of consciousness has been proposed, and its unrevisable core has been presented and defended. The journey inward must now pause for a moment to reflect on certain further aspects of cognitional process: that it is already engaged in; that it is fully natural; and that such natural engagement is its ultimate justification.

A Process Already Underway

From the start it has been emphasized that the world of inner experience is not some totally unknown territory to be explored. It is more like a neighborhood that one skirts or traverses all the time, without ever having fully investigated it. Common-sense awareness has already its practical knowledge of cognitional process; all that is lacking is a systematic cataloguing and organizing of what one was already at least dimly aware.

Much like the data of sense or of consciousness, then, cognitional process is itself a given; it exists long before one comes to pay explicit attention to it.

The German Existentialists have a nice word for this situation: *Geworfenheit*. The German word *werfen* means "to throw." Its past participle is *geworfen*, which means "thrown"; the *-heit*, like the English *-ness*, turns that into an abstract noun, so that it comes to mean literally, "thrownness." The German Existentialists used that word to characterize the human situation: we do not choose to be; we find ourselves already thrown into existence. No one asked our opinion; we are simply here, and have to make the best of it. Knowing is simply a particular case: we are thrown into knowing, without ever having been consulted about it. By the time we become explicitly aware of it, it is far too late to decide whether we want to become knowers or not; we already are.

One might question the Existentialist metaphor. Throwing is rather violent; we speak of someone as thrown into jail, which gives the sense of a fate, hard, unwilled, and resented. That may, indeed, have been the Existentialist attitude, but the story of Genesis has a gentler metaphor: man is placed in existence, is placed in fact in a garden; and woman is given to him for companionship.

In any case, whether we are thrown into knowing, or placed in it, the fact remains that our involvement in it precedes any choice on our part. We did not decide to become knowers; and when we become aware of the question, it is clearly too late to decide.

A Natural Involvement

The point has already been made that the desire to know is just as real, if less palpable, than hunger or the sex drive. As many dieters have discovered, one cannot simply choose not to be hungry; nor can a person just decide, I will never be sexually attracted to someone again. In much the same way, a person cannot say, I don't want to be a knower anymore.

Birds have to fly; fish have to swim. With much the same natural exigency, human beings have to ask questions, puzzle over things, see how they fit together, give them a universal expression, ask whether that expression captures what really is so, weigh the evidence, demand proof, and make probable and definitive judgments.

Even the person who would consider no longer being a knower would want to ponder the implications of that act first, conceive the alternatives, ask whether not knowing would be better than knowing, and weigh the options thoroughly, seeking good reasons before making such an important judgment. So native is intelligence and reasonableness to the human being that one would want to cease possessing those qualities only after being satisfied that it was the smart and reasonable thing to do.

The Ultimate Justification of Cognitional Process

Cognitional process, it has been maintained, is self-justifying, in that the very exercise of the activities involved makes their simultaneous denial incoherent. The further point to be noted here is that this is also their final justification: no further justification can be sought, and if it is sought, it will be done so incoherently. This must be briefly spelled out.

As seen above, involvement in cognitional process is, for the human knower, both already given and perfectly natural. To seek a deeper justification for it, one would have to use those mental activities, that already given involvement in the process. Just as one cannot use cognitional process, coherently, to deny cognitional process, so, equally, one cannot, coherently, use cognitional process to give a deeper foundation to cognitional process.

To demonstrate cognitional process one would have to frame a prospective judgment that human knowing has a more valid basis than that afforded by the simple engagement in the process. Then one would have to supply evidence for that prospective judgment. Note that one is using cognitional process to ground the conclusion. But the conclusion to be reached can never be firmer than the process itself used to reach it. Therefore the foundation for cognitional process can never be firmer than cognitional process itself.

A comparison might be made here to logic. It is well known that a conclusion can be no stronger than its premises. Conceive here, then, a super-logic, in which the ultimate premise is not any particular proposition, but cognitional process itself. No conclusion may be educed from that premise which is stronger than the premise itself. Thus it is incoherent to use cognitional process to give to it a deeper foundation than it already constitutes by its own active and self-justifying functioning.

To put the point another way, the process of knowing precedes the reflection on knowing. Thus common-sense awareness precedes the natural sciences, and the natural sciences precede the science of cognition. The science of consciousness can give definition and order to the process that precedes it. But it depends upon and assumes that prior process; it cannot, therefore, turn around and demonstrate it.

We are simply repeating a point already advanced: the journey inward is a journey of discovery, not a journey of creation. It does not bring into being the mental activities being investigated but recognizes them as landmarks, and situates them carefully in relation to one another. Inner data is a given for the interior scientist, just as sense data is a given for the physical scientist. It would make no more sense to ask the scientist of cognition to demonstrate the validity of cognitional process than it would to ask the natural scientist to demonstrate the existence of the physical world before beginning an investigation.

23

The Myth of Knowing as Looking

"Seeing is believing" is a common sentiment. It appears to reduce knowing to something as simple as physical sight. Both in common sense and, often, in philosophy itself, it presents itself as a simple alternative to the more complex structure of knowing that has been assembled in the preceding pages. It is the constant temptation of both common sense and philosophy to confuse what is most accessible in knowing—sense experience—with knowing itself. That is the myth of "knowing as looking."

It is not that seeing and the other senses have nothing to do with knowing. Indeed, as seen already, any knowledge of the outer world must begin in sense experience. The error comes when one takes that starting point as the whole.

Perhaps the most famous and economical presentation of that position is Bishop Berkeley's formula "esse est percipi": "being is being perceived," or, "to be is to be perceived." It would appear to locate knowing exclusively on the first level of cognitional process, the experiential; hence such a position is often called empiricism.

The natural correlate of empiricism is materialism. If only that exists which can be recognized by the senses, then the whole of reality is exhausted in the material. This too is a consistent inclination in philosophy, as it can be traced from the Greek materialists, notably Democritus, down to the materialism of Karl Marx. For this philosophical approach, all is matter; mind is but matter in motion.

Bishop Berkeley was not a simple materialist. He was also a Christian, and his philosophy was more sophisticated and paradoxical. Far from being a materialist, he is known in fact as an "immaterialist." Not only is being recognized by being perceived; in fact, that is all being is. There is, for Bishop Berkeley, no external world, only the perceiving itself.

Boswell tells a famous story about Samuel Johnson's reaction to Bishop Berkeley's theory:

> After we came out of the church, we stood talking for some time together of Bishop Berkeley's ingenious sophistry to prove the non-existence of matter, and that every thing in the universe is merely ideal. I observed, that though we are satisfied his doctrine is not true, it is impossible to refute it. I never shall forget the alacrity with which Johnson answered, striking his foot with mighty force against a large stone, till he rebounded from it, "I refute it thus" (James Boswell, *The Life of Samuel Johnson* in *Great Books of the Western World*, vol. 44 [Chicago: William Benton, 1952] 134).

This delightful tale may be read in one of two ways. In a more sophisticated way, what Johnson may be implying would be something like this: I am being asked for an assessment of the judgment that there is no external world. I perform an experiment, by which I exhibit that the external world, as instanced in this rock, is hard, and resistant, and unyielding. That experience is sufficient evidence to affirm the opposite judgment, that the external world does exist.

Perhaps that is being too kind to the good Dr. Johnson, however, who was not a trained philosopher. What he may have meant was simply, This rock is real, because I can feel it, because I can stub my toe against it. If so, then Johnson was in fact espousing the position that "seeing is believing": the criterion of true knowing is found simply in sense experience.

What is at stake, then, are two criteria of reality. In the simpler presentation, reality is just the object of sense experience. To know is to perceive with the senses. According to the more sophisticated position, knowing is the object of experience, insight, and judgment. What is known is affirmed with sufficient evidence. The simpler presentation has a certain plausibility. Knowing does usually begin in sense experience, and that experience is the element most easily recognizable in knowing. But that simple account is ultimately simplistic. It mistakes the part for the whole. Among other things, it would rule out any appeal to inner experience, which would make impossible any science of consciousness. More important, if carried through consistently, it would utterly exclude any spiritual reality, anything beyond the material.

Reality, then, is to be measured by the more sophisticated account of knowing that has been assembled. The real is not merely what is seen or perceived, but what is understood, and what is affirmed with sufficient evidence.

The empiricist account of knowing may be undermined by the simple expedient of questioning it. To ask what the empiricist philosophy means, or even to ask what this particular experience of seeing implies, is already to move to the level of understanding, and to leave behind the purely empirical. For if empiricism were true, there would be only experience, and questions would never arise. But once empiricism is questioned, the knower may then go on to understand it, discern its implications, and question whether or not it is true.

The knower cannot coherently affirm empiricism to be true, because the very act of affirming establishes that there is more to mental process and to knowing than simple experience.

Jesus is not usually thought of as an epistemologist. Yet there are epistemological implications to some of his statements. This is particularly true of a story toward the end of John's Gospel. Jesus appeared to his disciples on the night of Easter, but Thomas was not with them. When told of the encounter, Thomas was sceptical. He would not believe unless he could put his finger into Jesus' wounds. A week later, Jesus appears again, and Thomas is with the disciples. Jesus invites Thomas to do just as he had demanded, rebuking him for his disbelief. Thomas makes the profession of faith which forms the literary climax of the Gospel; but Jesus points up the moral of the story: "You became a believer because you saw me. Blest are they who have not seen and have believed" (John 20:9). Reality, then, is larger and grander than what can be seen. The gospel is diametrically opposed to any empiricism.

That same message may also be the deepest meaning of the myth of the cave. It concerns two criteria of reality. On the one hand, there is the criterion that most people adopt, the spontaneous empiricism that identifies knowing with experience. But such people are deceived. What they see are mere shadows, though they take them to be realities: "Do you not think they would suppose that in naming the things that they saw they were naming passing objects?" Again, what they heard were not true voices, but echoes: "And if their prison had an echo from the wall opposite them, when one of the passers-by uttered a sound, do you think that they would suppose anything else than the passing shadow to be the speaker?" In other words, the prisoners of the cave take shadows and echoes to be reality: "Then in every way such prisoners would deem reality to be nothing else than the shadows of artificial objects." Such a confusion is the natural human condition, Socrates implies. For when Glaucon confesses this to be a strange image, and these strange prisoners, Socrates says, "Like to us."

But there is a release and a healing to such confusion. It comes when the knower—perhaps against any natural inclinations—is freed from his shackles, allowed to turn around, and face the light itself. In this way he is able to approach reality in its true nature: "What do you suppose would be his answer if someone told him that what he had seen before was all a cheat and an illusion, but that now, being nearer to reality and turned toward more real things, he saw more truly?" The process is not easy, and the habituation would take time. But eventually the person would be able to see the sun, the very source of light, in its own reality: "And so, finally, I suppose he would be able to look upon the sun itself and see its true nature, not by reflections in water or phantasms of it in an alien setting, but in and by itself in its own place."

Almost all the terms for mental activities, it was pointed out in chapter 3, are taken from metaphors from sense experience. Thus "in-sight" means, literally, "looking into." Perhaps now the importance of this observation can be appreciated. Since sense experience is more obvious, and inner experience more hidden, this appeal is natural and appropriate; and it does no harm as long as it is kept in mind that the expression is metaphorical. The problems begin when the expression is taken literally. Then one falls into the empiricist trap of identifying knowing with looking, believing with seeing.

24

The Structure of Knowing and the History of Philosophy

In the chapter in which the reader was invited to affirm the structure of cognitional process, the question was raised whether other philosophers besides Lonergan have accounts of knowing. In fact many do; but once the basic structure is established, the question can be turned around: Are other accounts of knowing adequate? Thus the structure of knowing may exercise a critical function in assessing the history of philosophy. A few key instances which are particularly clear will be offered as illustrations of this possibility.

The Early Augustine

The move from materialism to a more adequate view of reality can be followed in Augustine's *Confessions*. He began with a position in which the only realities he recognized were bodily ones. If he thought of spiritual realities, he nevertheless could not imagine them except as bodies. He speaks of "spiritual things of which I was unable to think, except corporeally" (St. Augustine, *Confessions*, trans. Vernon J. Bourke, *The Fathers of the Church*, vol. 21 [New York: Fathers of the Church, 1953] Bk. VI, ch. 4, 6 [136]). Such a position is empiricist: the criterion of knowing is physical sight: "For, I was unable to think of any substance except that kind which is customarily seen through these eyes" (Bk. VIII, ch. 1, 1 [161]).

The result was materialism. What was not a body, what was not extended in space, simply did not exist at all. "Thus, in my grossness of mind (for I was not even able to gain a clear view of my very self), I thought that whatever was not extended through some spatial magnitude, or spread out, or formed into a mass, or puffed out—or took, or could take, such form—must be simply nothing" (Bk. VII, ch. 1, 2 [162]).

Augustine's first reading of the Old Testament had put him off, and convinced him that Christianity could not be true, because God is pictured there in human form (in Genesis, for example, God walks in the garden in the cool of the evening).

The sermons of Ambrose led him to a double breakthrough. First, Ambrose assured Augustine that the Old Testament statements were metaphorical, not literal. Second, he introduced Augustine to the notion of a reality that was fully spiritual—which was not a body, and nevertheless quite real.

> And I listened with joy to Ambrose, saying often in his sermons to the people, as though he were most carefully commending it as a rule: "the letter kills but the spirit gives life." When, having lifted the mystic veil, he laid bare the spiritual meaning of those things which seemed to teach error when taken literally, he said nothing that offended me . . . (Bk. VI, ch. 4, 6 [136]).

Augustine may be thought of as having taken an interior journey, discovering within himself an intelligence and a judgment that transcended sense experience, consequently arriving at a new criterion of reality.

> Thus, by a gradual process, from bodies to the soul which senses through the body, and thence to its interior power to which bodily sensation takes messages about exterior things (and this is as far as brutes can go), and then further to the reasoning power, to which what is taken by the bodily senses is brought for judgment (Bk. VIII, ch. 17, 23 [187]).

Descartes

That Descartes strongly emphasized the concept has already been remarked. In fact, that is an understatement, for Descartes saw in the clear and distinct concept the very criterion of truth. This realization came to him as a by-product of the "Cogito, ergo sum" argument. As he explains in the *Discourse on the Method of Rightly Conducting the Reason:*

> And having remarked that there was nothing at all in the statement "I think, therefore I am" which assures me of having thereby made a true assertion, excepting that I see very clearly that to think it is necessary to be, I come to the conclusion that I might assume, as a general rule, that the things which we conceive very clearly and distinctly are all true (From *The Philosophical Works of Descartes,* trans. Elizabeth S. Haldane and G. R. T. Ross [Cambridge, England: University Press, 1968] 1:102).

The same point is made even more forcefully in the *Meditations on the First Philosophy:*

> I am certain that I am a thing which thinks; but do I not then like-
> wise know what is requisite to render me certain of a truth? Certainly
> in this first knowledge there is nothing that assures me of its truth,
> excepting the clear and distinct perception of that which I state, which
> would not indeed suffice to assure me that what I say is true, if it
> could ever happen that a thing which I conceived so clearly and dis-
> tinctly could be false; and accordingly it seems to me that already
> I can establish that as a general rule that all things which I perceive
> very clearly and very distinctly are true (Ibid., 1:158).

Descartes cannot be called an empiricist, then, in that he goes beyond
the level of experience to that of understanding, by placing the criterion
of truth in the concept. On the other hand, his account of cognition is
still partial, for he overlooks the level of reflection, and the key contribution of judgment.

Kant

Kant's position is somewhat more complicated: he appears to combine the empiricist account of the early Augustine with the conceptual
stress of Descartes. Kant uses the term *intuition*, but what he has in mind
is sense perception:

> Knowledge involves two factors: first, the concept, through which
> an object in general is thought (the category); and secondly, the intu-
> ition, through which it is given. For if no intuition could be given
> corresponding to the concept, the concept would still indeed be a
> thought, so far as its form is concerned, but would be without any
> object, and no knowledge of anything would be possible by means
> of it . . . (Immanuel Kant, *Critique of Pure Reason*, trans. Norman
> Kemp Smith [New York: St. Martin's, 1963] B146 [161–62]).
> Our knowledge springs from two fundamental sources of the mind;
> the first is the capacity of receiving representations (receptivity for
> impressions), the second is the power of knowing an object through
> these representations (spontaneity of concepts). Through the first an
> object is given to us, through the second the object is thought in rela-
> tion to that representation (which is a mere determination of the mind).
> Intuition and concepts constitute, therefore, the elements of all our
> knowledge, so that neither concepts without an intuition in some way
> corresponding to them, nor intuition without concepts, can yield
> knowledge (B74 [92]).

He summarizes this with an aphoristic brevity: "Thoughts without content are empty, intuitions without concepts are blind" (B75 [93]).

Though Kant, as well as Descartes, is often called an idealist, because of his stress on concepts, there are also ways in which, insisting on the double criterion of concept and sense experience, he remains an empiricist. He rules out most metaphysical questions as illegitimate, precisely because they are beyond the physical, that is, beyond sense experience or intuition. In this regard his position is the same as the early Augustine's: nothing can be real if it is not a body.

Thomas Aquinas

To find an adequate stress on judgment, one must go back to medieval philosophers. Thomas Aquinas, in particular, places a strong emphasis on judgment as the single criterion of truth.

Thomas's argument begins with the definition of truth: it is the conformity of mind with reality. So to know truth is to know that conformity. It is not enough to *be* in conformity with reality, then; one must also *know* the conformity. But the senses, though they may *be* in conformity with reality, do not *know* the conformity: hence truth is not to be sought there. Again, an insight or a concept may *be* in conformity with reality; but it does not *know* that conformity, for the question has not yet arisen, Is that true? The conformity of mind and reality is only *known*, then, in judgment.

Here is the way that Thomas himself explains it:

> Truth, as we have said, is, in its primary significance, in the intellect. Now since a thing is true as having the form proper to its own nature, it must follow that the mind, in the act of knowing, is true as having the likeness of the thing known, which is the form of the intellect in the act of knowing. Accordingly truth is defined as conformity between intellect and thing. Hence to know that conformity is to know truth. Sense however does not know that conformity in any way; for although sight possesses the likeness of the visible thing, it does not know the correspondence between the thing and what it apprehends about it. Intellect can know its own conformity to the thing known; yet it does not grasp that conformity in the mere act of knowing the essence of a thing. But when the intellect judges that the thing corresponds to the form of the thing which it apprehends then for the first time it knows and affirms truth. . . . Therefore properly speaking truth is in the intellect in its function of affirming and denying one reality of another; and not in sense, nor in intellect knowing the meaning (Thomas Aquinas, *Summa theologiae* 1.16.2 [London: Blackfriars, 1963] 81).

Conclusion

The illustrations have been few, and highly selective. But perhaps enough has been said to suggest how one might construct a whole history of philosophy from the critical standpoint of the structure of consciousness. As there are three levels of cognition, so there would also be three basic philosophical approaches, depending on where the emphasis is placed, and where the criterion of truth is located:

Judgment	Realism
Insight	Idealism
Experience	Empiricism

Such categories are rarely encountered in such pure forms. As this brief survey has already indicated, actual philosophical positions will consist of some variation or combination of one or more of these basic possibilities. Nevertheless, the schema is helpful in organizing the profusion of philosophical stances.

25

Metaphysics: The Structure of the Known

Our journey into the inner world of consciousness proceeded through a discovery of various mental activities, culminating in an affirmation of cognitional structure. That affirmation was seen to be self-justifying, and the structure, once established, has led to a variety of insights. The structure of knowing was found to be echoed in scientific method, as experience was correlated with data gathering, insight with framing hypotheses, and judgment with the crucial experiment. But the structure of knowing was also seen to ground an intellectual morality: experience suggested the imperative, Be attentive; insight, Be intelligent; and the structure of judgment, Be judicious. In the last chapter, the structure of knowing was also seen to provide a critical framework for the history of philosophy, where every position would be some variation or combination of the possibilities of empiricism (criterion of truth in experience), idealism (criterion of truth in insight or concept), or realism (criterion of truth in judgment). The question therefore arises, Does the structure of knowing say anything about the structure of the known?

By and large, it does not. As the foregoing investigation suggests, knowing arises from particular experiences. They cannot be predicted in advance, but must be awaited "a posteriori," as Kant would say. I cannot predict what experiences I will have today; I will have to wait to see what the day brings. As the experiences are particular, so the insights that arise from them will also be particular. Nor is the result of the level of understanding more predictable. How intelligent will I be in dealing with the experiences I have? Will my direction of attention close off certain insights? Will my past ignorance prevent me from present discovery? Are there perhaps things I would rather not understand? Judgment rests upon insight, and is just as unpredictable as insight. It also presents its own sources of uncertainties: if I am a rash judger, the judgment will take place without proper evidence, and will likely be mistaken; and if I am too hesitant, I might not even make a judgment that is reasonable and sufficiently grounded.

Yet this largely negative—and quite accurate—assessment of the predictability of knowing does suggest that whatever I know, however particular, will be known by the same process of experiencing it, understanding it, and judging it. Does that not imply something invariable about what is to be known?

Perhaps the point may be made clearer by appeal to the metaphor of a key and a lock. A key and a lock are designed to match one another. A key is meant to open one lock, and not others; while a lock is similarly designed to be opened by a specific designed key, and not others. Given a lock, a locksmith can craft a key to fit it; given a key, he or she can tell what kind of lock it would fit; given enough time, a skilled locksmith could probably even manufacture the corresponding lock.

Suppose, then, that knowing is a key. What is the lock that it would fit?

Immediately one realizes that knowing is a very flexible sort of thing, that can know ever so many different kinds of things. So perhaps one must at once modify the metaphor to make of knowing a master key, even the master key of all master keys. But even a master key, which can fit many locks, still has some kind of structure. So it should be possible to say something about the lock—that is, about the known. If knowing were completely shapeless, one could infer nothing about the known. But, as seen already, knowing does have a definite structure, which was investigated in the early chapters of this work, formulated in chapter 17, and affirmed in chapter 19.

If knowing, therefore, always begins in experience, then the known will always be somehow experience-able. If experience leads to insight, then the known must also be understandable, or intelligible. And if insight is completed only by the commitment of judgment, then the known has to be also affirmable. This may be summarized in a diagram:

Structure of Knowing	Structure of Known
Judgment	Affirmable
Insight	Intelligible
Experience	Experience-able

As these terms are rather cumbersome, it will be helpful to substitute a better nomenclature. Let the intelligible element in knowing be called *form*. That is an appropriate term, since insight is the grasping of pattern in a previously unorganized set of data. The *experience-able* may be called *potency*, since at the level of experience the question has not yet been asked, much less has an insight occurred, so that data as such constitutes only the possibility of knowing. Finally, let the *affirmable* be called *existence*, because it corresponds to judgment, which pronounces what is the case, what truly is so. That results in the following formulation:

Structure of Knowing	Structure of Known
Judgment	Existence
Insight	Form
Experience	Potency

If the key, then, has the shape of experience-insight-judgment, then the lock has the shape of potency-form-existence.

Note that potency, form, and existence are not three distinct things, as if by experience we know one thing, by insight another, and by judgment a third. The activities of knowing are not isolated, but are intimately related to each other: experience evokes insight, which leads to judgment; conversely, judgment is impossible without a prior insight, and insight without a prior experience. It is precisely what is experienced that may also be understood; and what is understood is precisely the same as what is affirmed—because judgment adds no more than a yes or no to insight or concept. But if what is experienced is what is understood is what is affirmed, and if knowing is the key to the lock of the known, then what is in potency on the level of experience is what is grasped as form on the level of intelligence is what is affirmed as existing on the level of judgment. In sum, if the elements of knowing constitute a single structure, then the elements of the known must also constitute a single structure.

In chapter 12 we saw that we do not experience the world as discrete atoms, which are then assembled into molecules, cells, plants, and animals; rather we experience first what were called *units*, which may later, by scientific analysis, be broken down into their components. In passing it was noted that these units possess *characteristics*. Thus parents may be tall or short, angry or smiling; dogs characteristically bark "bow-wow"; birds fly and fish swim; trees turn green and red, grow, and die; planets move in elliptical paths; and pendulums swing.

Without making any elaborate investigation into ordinary language, it may be noted that the units are normally denoted by nouns, and the characteristics by verbs or adjectives. This structure appears in-built into the English language, so that it is hard to violate. Take the last example: the pendulum swings. It is possible to take the verb and make it into an abstract noun, swinging. But while "the pendulum swings" makes perfect sense, the "swinging pendulums" is nonsense. Again, "the tree grows" makes sense; but "the growing takes place treely" does not.

Again, a more technical language may be helpful. Let the units be called *substance*, and the characteristics, *accidents*. A word must be said first about the term *substance*. It comes from the Latin *sub-stare*, "to stand under." In other words, it is metaphorically equivalent to "to under-stand." What must be kept in mind is that substance, like understanding, is a metaphor. To forget that, and take it literally, is to make a muddle.

The term *substance* has often been the subject of ridicule in modern philosophy. It was taken literally to mean to "stand under." The supposition was that substance was somehow "standing under" the reality of something; so that if one could strip off enough of the upper layers, one could eventually arrive at the "substance" "standing under" it. But since that idea is ludicrous, the idea of substance was also thought to be ridiculous.

The reason for this confusion may also be clear. Like the early Augustine, much of modern philosophy is empiricist. But for the empiricist, there is only body. So, if there is substance, it too must be a body. And since substance is not immediately visible, it must be a body inside the visible body.

This confusion can be avoided, however, if it is remembered that substance is not a body, but a unity. Furthermore, it is a unity, not as experienced, but as understood and affirmed. On the empirical level there is only a potential unity; for it is insight which grasps the unity, and judgment which affirms it. When the child on the train says, "Look, Mama, a cow!" he is grasping a substantial unity, understanding at once that this is a unity within the visual field of his experience, and that this unity is identical to those seen in previous pastures. On empiricist presuppositions, therefore, substance is a ridiculous notion; but on realist premises, it corresponds to the way we know.

Accident may be introduced more expeditiously. It takes its name from the fact that some characteristics are accidental to the substance. A tree may have green leaves in the spring, and red and yellow leaves in the fall; but no one supposes it is a different tree. The color of the leaves is accidental to the substance of the tree.

The structure of knowing may then be applied to the structure of the known in the light of this division. A substance may be experienced, understood, and affirmed; and an accident may be experienced, understood, and affirmed. Once more, the unity on the side of the knowing is reflected in a unity on the side of the known: sense experiences present the potential unity which is understood in the formal unity which is affirmed as the substantial existence; likewise the accident as experienced leads to the accident as understood to the accident as affirmed. Allowing for the distinction of substance and accident, then, the resulting structure of the known may be diagrammed as follows:

Structure of Knowing	Structure of Known	
Judgment	Substantial Existence	Accidental Existence
Insight	Substantial Form	Accidental Form
Experience	Substantial Potency	Accidental Potency

Anyone familiar with the history of philosophy will no doubt recognize this as the traditional Aristotelian and Thomistic metaphysics. Aristotle first distinguished substance and accident, and matter and form. Thomas distinguished more clearly existence and form.

What is novel in the approach to metaphysics being outlined here, however, is that the elements are being derived "scientifically." They are a derivation, in other words, from the new science of cognition. As such, they have an empirical base. As scientific terms arise from a study of sense experience, so these metaphysical terms arise out of a consideration of the inner experience of consciousness. Yet as the basic terms of the science of consciousness, unlike those of the physical sciences, are unrevisable, so will the metaphysical basic terms be unrevisable. What an approach to metaphysics through the structure of knowing, consequently, adds to Aristotelian and Thomistic metaphysics is an independent confirmation of their intuitive metaphysical genius, an empirical basis, and a promise of unrevisability.

Discussion so far has focused on "the known," but it can be seen immediately that it applies as well to "the knowable." Not only has everything already known arisen through the process of experiencing, understanding, and judging, but—unless the very structure of human knowing is changed—everything to be known by human beings will be known because it is experienced, understood, and affirmed, and therefore as potency, form, and existence, in its substantial and accidental forms.

Thus is revealed a paradox of the inner journey. It began as a journey inward, to discover the mental activities taking place within consciousness. It began also as a personal journey, because one has a unique and inalienable access to one's own consciousness. Yet it has been pursued now to the point where it becomes also an outer journey, which grasps not the details, but the basic structure of all that has been known, and predicts not the particularities, but the basic shape of everything to-be-known. And the journey which began as a personal quest has also arrived at a basic structure true of all human knowing and of all the human known: what has been known in the past, what is known in the present, and will ever be known in the future.

Envoi: One

Most books end with a conclusion; but the present text has been so much of a personal journey that a farewell seems more in order.

The original aim has been accomplished: to offer an accessible introduction to the leading ideas of Lonergan's *Insight*. The reader is now invited and urged to tackle the work itself. It will not, of course, be easy. But working through the present text should at least have prepared the reader to recognize the main themes of the book.

In the course of pursuing this project, some possibilities have also occurred to me of relatively more accessible ways to present some of the later chapters of *Insight*. Something similar appears to have happened in the composition of the book itself. In an interview Lonergan describes it this way:

> When I had that much done, I could see people all around saying, "Well, if you have this sort of position you can't have a metaphysics." So I thought I'd be safer to put in four more chapters on metaphysics.
>
> "Well, you can't have an ethics," so I put in a chapter on that.
>
> And, "You can't prove the existence of God," so I put a chapter on that.
>
> Then, "What has this to do with your being a priest?" So I put a little bit on religion in Chapter XX—a moving viewpoint! (Bernard J. F. Lonergan, *A Second Collection* [Philadelphia: Westminster 1974] 222).

Hence chapters will be added here on morality, being, God, and a final chapter on wisdom. These may be thought of as an encore to the main performance, and the audience is free to leave or to remain. The reader who stays, however, should be warned that in the following chapters the ground will be covered more rapidly, and the way will become rockier and steeper.

For those who have followed loyally to this point, and feel they have achieved their purpose, what occurs to me is the Latin word "vale!" It is a farewell which means something like, "Be well! Be strong!" My best wishes go with the reader on his or her continued journey of discovery and self-discovery.

26

Knowing and Morality

The inner journey has been seen as a way to illuminate not only the structure of knowing, but also the history of philosophy and the structure of the known. The question of this chapter is whether such an approach has anything to say about morality. As much as possible, parallels will be stressed with what has been done already.

An intellectual morality has already been discussed: Be attentive, be intelligent, and, above all, do not make judgments without proper evidence. But now the investigation must widen to include a larger morality. Chapters 13 and 14 have already called attention to a unique object of our knowing: we know not only what is already the case, but we make judgments also about future actions. These are the stuff of promises, contracts, vows, etc. Future human actions constitute the field of morality.

Such a reflection reveals how narrow, to this point, the inner investigation of consciousness has been. If it has said a great deal about knowing, it has said practically nothing about acting, doing, choosing. Still another uninvestigated field is that of feelings. They are so many and so complex they might call for a book in themselves.

For present purposes, however, the contrast of knowing and doing is the more significant one. That has already been represented by the figures of Mary and Martha in the gospel story. Mary stands for contemplation, knowing; Martha is the figure of action. It is Martha on whom attention must now focus.

Action itself, however, may be divided into outer and inner. What is visible are the external actions Martha performs: setting the table, peeling the vegetables, baking the bread. Those actions are not negligible in moral analysis, and eventually consideration would have to return to them. But a morality that is parallel to the inner journey into knowing must concentrate first and foremost on the inner presuppositions and determinants of that outer action.

External action follows upon human desire. It is, indeed, the prior act of choosing which renders a human action moral. Some things we do unconsciously. Others we do unthinkingly, or by spontaneous reaction. Some actions we may be forced into, or tricked into. But those are only of peripheral interest to morality. It is what we do knowingly and by free choice that forms the central interest of moral analysis.

When one turns from the outer world of action to the inner world of willing and choosing, one finds the reality to be more complex than would perhaps be expected. As there are a number of mental activities that constitute knowing, so is there also a plurality that constitutes choosing. In fact, *choosing* itself is too narrow a word, and it may be better to begin with a more undifferentiated *desiring*.

Another notion that must be introduced is that of the *good*, which may be defined as the object of desire. Since the focus here is on human action and its moral analysis, that desire may be understood as human desire, though later a more comprehensive definition may be sought. The human good, then, is the object of human desire.

The good is itself knowable; as already seen, one object of human knowing is the range of possible human actions. But that suggests, since from the structure of knowing we can already predict something of the known, that we can grasp already the structure of the good. The good must be, first, the subject of experience; call it the *felt good*. Second, that same good must be intelligible. Since human actions are in question, the action being analyzed will be an intelligent and intelligible solution to a human situation. This is the good as form, order, system, organization. Third, the action in question must be judged to be fully reasonable, to be a true value. The knowledge of the good may therefore be summarized as follows:

Judgment	Affirmable good—good of value
Insight	Intelligible good—good of order
Experience	Experiential good—felt good

When one turns to the analysis of desire, one finds something of this same complexity. As in philosophy the basic dichotomy was between empiricism and realism, between the criterion of what is seen and felt versus what is understood and affirmed, so is there a duality of desire. On the experiential level is what might be called *sensual desire*, for the good as felt. On the level of judgment is what may be termed *intellectual* or *spiritual desire*, the desire for value, for what truly is the reasonable thing to do in a situation.

Those two desires ground two possible criteria of morality. One is the morality of the felt good. Its criterion is, "If it feels good, do it." Its calculus is one of pleasures and pains. Pleasure is to be sought; pain is to be avoided. Over against this is a morality based on the understood and affirmed good. Its motto is, "If it's truly reasonable, do it." This is a morality based on value.

Not surprisingly, the two moralities diverge. There are times when the pleasurable action is not a reasonable one, and there are also times when the reasonable action requires the endurance of labor, hardship, and pain.

As the fruit of a long analysis of knowing was a distinction of sensing and judging, and a determination that sensing was not to be ignored—it is the beginning of knowing—but to be acknowledged as a partial component of knowing, so a mature moral analysis accepts that pleasures and pains are not to be simply ignored—they represent partial goods and evils—but must be subordinated to the larger criterion of the intelligible and the reasonable.

Morality may be thought of, then, as the extension of knowing into doing. The commitment of the morally mature person is to do what is truly reasonable in every situation.

What must also be recognized, however, is that there is a gap between knowing and doing. To know what is the reasonable action is not automatically to do it. Anyone who is at all morally reflective is aware that one can know perfectly well what should be done, and still not do it. This represents one of the key differences between the moral philosophies of Plato and Aristotle. Plato tended to place everything in the education of the mind: if people understand what is the right thing, they will do it. Without denying the importance of knowing, Aristotle insisted that another element was necessary: a moral training of choosing and willing. But the person who best grasped the gap between knowing and doing was Paul. As he says in the Letter to the Romans: "I cannot even understand my own actions. I do not do what I want to do but what I hate. . . . What happens is that I do, not the good I will to do, but the evil I do not intend" (Rom 7:15-19).

The key to moral development, then, is to bridge that gap between knowing and doing, to bring a theoretical knowledge to actual and effective performance. Toward this end Aristotle saw habits, or virtues, as crucial. It has been noted that when an insight occurs, it marks a breakthrough. What was once difficult, seemingly impossible, now seems easy. What is once understood can be grasped again, either immediately, or at least with much less effort the second time. A habit of virtue marks a similar breakthrough in the moral field. Once one has become habituated to a good action, it becomes easier, even pleasurable, to perform.

Growth in moral maturity, then, is largely a training in virtuous habits; and teaching morality will be largely a matter of teaching virtue. That is a topic, it will be remembered, that Socrates was already vitally interested in.

Another parallel may be traced. As there is an inborn drive to know, so is there also a native desire for the good. As the drive to know must be nurtured in informal conversation and formal schooling, so must the natural desire for the good be strengthened and directed. But neither desire needs to be created—nor can it be. If one evinces no drive to know at all, one will remain an imbecile. And without any desire for the good, one would be a social psychopath.

Further, as the drive to know provides a criterion to reinforce or exclude any formulated structure of knowing, so does the native desire for the good constitute an original moral compass against which any particular moral system may be measured. This point needs to be spelled out somewhat.

To recapitulate briefly, the drive to know unfolds in a structure of mental activities. Once those activities are correctly formulated, that formulation is self-justifying, because it is in keeping with the underlying activities necessary to discover and affirm it. But any partial account of cognitional structure, such as empiricism or idealism, is incoherent. It is not that such an account is necessarily contradictory in itself; it is rather that it is incoherent with the very activities of experiencing, understanding, and judging which were necessary to elaborate and affirm it.

Something similar is true within morality. The desire for the good unfolds on the two levels of the felt good and the reasonable good. Once these goods are distinguished, and a person is committed to the pursuit of the reasonable good, there is a potential for moral development. Any action that is unreasonable, then, is in conflict with growth toward moral maturity. Further, any account of morality that falls short of the criterion of reasonable action is also, by that very fact, incompatible with the direction given by that moral compass which is the native desire for the truly good. Hedonism says that pleasure is the supreme law of human action. As a moral philosophy, it may not be contradictory in itself; but it becomes incoherent as soon as one maintains that it is the reasonable guide for human action. For to do so at once implicitly affirms, while explicitly denying, the criterion of reasonable value.

Everything said so far may be summarized in the major precept of morality, Do good and avoid evil, where good is the truly reasonable action, and evil is the unreasonable action. That may seem cruelly general, to the point of being almost useless. But as the inner journey yields in metaphysics only the general structure of the known, without determining any particulars, so the present account of morality must be content with this general precept. As filling in the particulars of knowing requires the patient application to the world without of experience, insight, and judgment, so the discovery of particular moral codes requires a patient investigation of human situations, the weighing of the merits of various possible courses of action, and so on.

Nevertheless, the person setting out on the road to moral maturity does not have to try to begin from scratch. As the student who wants to fill in the particulars of the known can fall back on a long history of human knowing, so is there also a rich tradition of moral knowing in the human community, the fruit of centuries of acute moral analysis and of fidelity to the native desire for the truly good.

The moral student must, however, be wary. Not everything in popular morality flows from a true ideal; much has come from the temptation of pleasure and the easy compromise. It will be necessary always to test the received moral tradition against one's own inner moral compass. Thus will the wisdom of age make common cause with the irrepressible idealism of youth.

Above all, the person in pursuit of moral maturity should not anticipate an easy task. A twofold requirement imposes itself: first, to discover what is the truly reasonable; second—and more difficult—to bridge the gap between knowing and doing by the cultivation of virtue, until doing the reasonable thing in every situation becomes easy, assured, almost instinctive. To achieve this it will be necessary to face one's own moral failures; to steel oneself against the siren call of pleasure, and harden oneself to the pains that will accompany following always the commitment to value.

At the very beginning the reader was warned that the inner journey would not be easy. As it progresses, its difficulties and demands become more and more apparent.

27

Being: The Object of the Pure Desire to Know

In this and the following chapters the focus of the inward journey will move toward totality. The attempt will be only to suggest how the ideas mentioned may be arrived at; for a full argumentation the reader is referred to Lonergan's *Insight*.

Chapter 25 showed that the structure of the known, as potency, form, and existence, applied not merely to all that is known, but to everything knowable. The totality of everything known and knowable is being.

The same idea may be approached in a number of ways. Being is everything about which one can ask in a well-formed, legitimate question. The qualification of "well-formed" or "legitimate" is necessary because, as was seen in connection with inverse insight, a question may be mistaken in its very presuppositions. In that case there is no intelligible answer to it; such a question does not intend being.

Again, being is all that can be understood. The intelligible form corresponding to every insight is an aspect of being; every correct insight grasps some element of being; and being as a whole is the object of all possible insights into the intelligible.

Once more, being is all that can be affirmed as existing. Every true affirmation concerns some component of being; and the totality of all true judgments would bear on being as a whole.

But, as already clarified, the desire to know is the source of every particular question, every particular insight, every particular judgment; and it moves on from any particular judgment to raise new questions, heading toward new insights and new judgments. Most simply and comprehensively, then, being may be defined as the object of the pure desire to know.

What is especially notable about this idea of being is that it is all-embracing, all-inclusive. What is outside of being is literally "no-thing."

This last affirmation may be doubted. What if there is some X which is beyond being? But one has only to ask, What is X?, and it is seen to be included in the desire to know. Suppose, however, there is some limit to human knowing. Then being will be limited. But then, one only has to ask, What is beyond the limit? and once again being includes the limited, the limit, and what goes beyond it.

On the other hand, it may be objected, being is too inclusive. After all, there are such things as illegitimate questions. The drive to know, however, precedes any formulated questions, because it is the drive to know which raises all questions. The drive to know is not interested in the answers to illegitimate questions, because they are unintelligible, and knowing is a matter of understanding and judging. But note, further, that it is also precisely the drive to know that will distinguish and separate invalid from valid questions.

Again, it may be objected, being is too inclusive because no one can ask and answer all questions. There are many questions a knower will be simply uninterested in; and even were a knower interested in every question, life is short, and each answer requires a discrete amount of time.

No doubt, there is a proper order to posing questions. Children want the answers to all questions at once. The student gradually discovers that some questions must be answered before others can usefully be asked and answered. To hold some questions in abeyance while answering others is not necessarily to say the other questions are foolish or useless or illegitimate; it is simply to put them off until they can effectively be answered. But being includes the answers to both the proximate and the remote questions.

Again, the ideal of the natural sciences, for example, involves complete explanation for all physical phenomena. That does not mean that any particular scientist, or the scientists of any particular time, will achieve that ideal. But being, which embraces every area of knowing, is measured by the ideal, not by present achievement. Being, in other words, is not defined by what is known; it is the totality of the known and the knowable.

Because being has been defined as the object of all correct insights, it is clear that all being is intelligible. Everything that exists, then, is in some way intelligible, the object of a possible insight; and the absolutely unintelligible is nothing.

The last chapter dealt with the good, but the good in a limited sense, the good of morality, or of possible future human actions. But the move to a totality here suggests the possibility of a cosmic account of the good. If all being is intelligible, is all being good?

Within the field of human knowing, the intelligible and the good were seen to be co-terminous. Every good possible course of action was also an intelligible solution to a human situation. It is only necessary to suppose, then, that every intelligible is likewise good.

This supposition can be bolstered by considering the alternatives. Is it possible that the good is more comprehensive than being? But then there would be an X outside of the pure desire to know. Ask what that X is, and it is included in the desire to know. So the good cannot be more inclusive than being.

Could being, then, be more inclusive than the good? The good has been defined as the object of desire. One kind of desire, however, is the desire to know. Now any being can be the object of the desire to know, because being is precisely the object of the desire to know. Therefore the desirable cannot be less extensive than the knowable, and so being cannot extend beyond the good.

If the good cannot be more inclusive than being, and being cannot be more inclusive than the good, then being and the good must be co-terminous.

In the last chapter a parallel was made between knowing and willing, and that suggests a further argument. The drive to know goes beyond any limits; if the parallel holds, then the will's desire for good also goes beyond any limits. And that seems to be the case. The human desire for good appears to be insatiable. No one ever seems to come to the point of being perfectly satisfied, of having enough; always there appears some fly in the ointment, which allows for further improvement. As it is popularly said, "You can never be thin enough or rich enough." As the drive to know seeks an unlimited intelligible, then, so the desire for the good seeks an unlimited good. Thus the intelligible and the good are co-terminous. But the intelligible and being are co-terminous. Therefore being and the good are also co-terminous.

Such a conclusion is in keeping with medieval philosophy, which held that being and the good are convertible. But it is also affirmed by the wisdom of Genesis, which records: "God looked at everything he had made, and he found it very good" (1:31).

The foregoing treatment of being suggests a further aspect of intellectual morality: the desire to know should be as wide as being. That does not mean that any human being can hope to know everything. Nor does it mean that everyone should investigate in every field, because there is a legitimate division of labor in the human collaboration of knowing. Nor does it mean that there is not a strategy to learning, for some questions are rightly postponed until others are answered. But it does mean that the discoveries of others are to be prized along with one's own; and it does mean that no legitimate question should be brushed aside as simply uninteresting, worthless, or foolish.

28

The Idea of God

The journey inward has, perhaps surprisingly, also illuminated the structure of the known, the history of philosophy, and the field of morality. Does it shed any light on the question of God? In keeping with the distinction between insight and judgment, the question will be dealt with in two parts, in this chapter and the following: Can God be understood? Can God be affirmed to exist?

As an approach to the understanding of God, postulate an insight adequate to being.

Such an insight will be the answer to all possible questions, because being has been defined as the object of all legitimate questions. Hence this insight will leave no question unanswered. Further, such an insight will unify in itself all possible insights, because being has been defined as the object of all possible insights into the intelligible, and this insight is adequate to being. Hence this insight will leave nothing unexplained, nothing which is not understood.

This insight will be one. Were it multiple, either one of the multiple insights would be adequate to being, or none would be. If one of the multiple insights is adequate to being, then the others are superfluous. But if none is adequate to being, then there is no insight adequate to being, which contradicts the original postulate. Therefore the insight adequate to being will be single.

The insight adequate to being will be simple. For were it composed of parts, these parts would represent partial understandings of being. But a partial understanding of being is not adequate to being, which contradicts the original postulate. Therefore the insight adequate to being will be simple.

The insight adequate to being will also be independent. It will depend on no further insights, because otherwise it would not be adequate to all of being. It will depend on no further intelligibles, because it grasps in itself all intelligibility, and leaves nothing which is not understood.

The insight adequate to being will be perfect. For the perfect is that which lacks nothing. But the insight adequate to being lacks no understanding. Therefore it is perfect understanding.

The insight adequate to being will be unlimited. For being was seen to transcend all possible limits, and this insight is adequate to being.

The unlimited insight will be spiritual. The idea of the spiritual, as opposed to the material, was discussed in connection with Augustine's conversion. Now it may be more carefully defined: the spiritual is the intelligent. As the level of intelligence goes beyond the level of experience, so the intellectual transcends the sensible, the spiritual transcends the physical, true value transcends the felt good. But the insight adequate to being is unlimited in intelligence, and so it is spiritual.

Human beings at once understand, and have bodies; therefore they are composed of the spiritual and the material. But the unlimited insight cannot have a body, because the unlimited insight is simple, not composed.

The unlimited insight is also timeless. For time is the measure of motion in a body, and the unlimited insight has no body. Nor can the unlimited insight grow in insight, as human beings do, because the unlimited insight already understands everything intelligible.

The unlimited insight is self-explanatory. The self-explanatory is what needs nothing else for full explanation. But if the unlimited insight needed something else for full explanation, it would require a further insight or a further intelligible. But that has already been ruled out. Therefore the unlimited insight is self-explanatory.

The unlimited insight is also judgment. Since the unlimited insight answers all questions, it answers not only all questions for understanding, but also all questions for reflection. As it understands everything, it grasps also the sufficiency of evidence to affirm itself as self-explanatory. Hence the unlimited insight is judgment as well as insight.

Further, this act of judgment is not other than this act of insight, for otherwise the judgment would constitute an intelligibility beyond the unlimited insight, on which the unlimited insight would be dependent. But such a dependence has already been excluded.

It follows that the unlimited insight is identical with a perfect judgment. It further follows that the unlimited insight is omniscient; as knowing reaches its culmination in judgment, so the unlimited insight knows everything about everything.

The unlimited insight understands itself. For if the unlimited insight understands everything about everything, then it certainly, and in the first instance, understands itself.

Further, the understanding and the understood in the unlimited insight are one. For were they two, then the unlimited insight would be composite, and, as already seen, it is simple.

Here the difference of cognitional theories becomes significant. In the myth of knowing as looking, knowing is an ultimate duality, including the looker and the looked-at. The looker is not in a good position to look at the looker. But if knowing is defined as insight and judgment, the situation is quite different. Understanding can understand itself; judging can affirm judging. This was called the boomerang effect: the activities of knowing return upon themselves. In the human being that return is not total. Performative contradiction is still possible; one may, however incoherently, make a judgment that judgment does not exist. But in the unlimited insight that return is total, to the point of identity: the understanding is one with the understood, the judger is one with the judgment and the judged. Knowing is, in the ultimate analysis, not duality, but unity.

The development to this point may recall Aristotle's idea of the Self-thinking Thought.

The unlimited insight is therefore the Primary Insight. If any other insights exist, they will constitute some pale reflection of the timeless "eureka" of the unlimited insight. The unlimited insight is also the Primary Intelligible. If any other intelligibilities exist, then they will be some remote participation in the Primary Intelligible. (Once more, the Primary Insight and the Primary Intelligible are not two, but one.)

But are there any other intelligibles? The inquiry appears to have boxed itself into a corner. On the one hand, there must be other intelligibles. At the very least, the present situation requires a writer, a reader, a book, and a postulation. And obviously, neither the writer, nor the reader, nor the book, nor the postulation is the Primary Insight. On the other hand, it has also been held that the Primary Insight cannot be dependent on any intelligibles outside itself. So how can this dilemma be resolved? If the Primary Insight does not understand other intelligibles, then it would be deficient in understanding, and not adequate to being. On the other hand, if it understands the other intelligibles, then it must need them for full understanding. Or is one to deny that the writer, the reader, the book, and the postulation are in any way intelligible?

The question is answered by pointing out that, if there are any intelligibles other than the Primary Intelligible, the Primary Insight understands them by understanding the Primary Intelligible. In other words, in understanding itself the Primary Insight understands also the various ways in which it may be reflected in other intelligibles. Hence it understands the other intelligibles without being dependent on them.

Consider now the following schema, familiar already from the journey into consciousness and the structure of the known.

| Judgment | Existence |
| Insight | Form |

Form is what is grasped by insight; it is another word for the intelligible. But the Primary Insight is one with the Primary Intelligible; in the Primary Insight, accordingly, insight is identical with form. That may be represented as follows:

| Judgment | | Existence |
| Insight | Equals | Form |

But it has also been shown that the Primary Insight is one with its act of judgment. Hence:

Judgment		Existence
Equals		
Insight	Equals	Form

It has also been argued that, in the Primary Insight, knower and known are one. Therefore the judger and the affirmed are one. But what is affirmed is existence. Therefore the judgment and the existence it affirms are one in the Primary Insight.

Judgment	Equals	Existence
Equals		
Insight	Equals	Form

If insight is one with form, judgment one with existence, and insight one with judgment, then it follows that, in the Primary Insight, form will be one with existence.

Judgment	Equals	Existence
Equals		Equals
Insight	Equals	Form

In more traditional terminology, the essence and the existence of the Primary Insight are identical. In other words, it is the very nature of the Primary Insight to exist.

If the Primary Insight is one with form, and its form one with existence, then the Primary Insight is also one with its Existence. And this coheres with what has been said already; for were the Primary Insight one thing and its Existence another, then the Primary Insight would be composite, not simple.

If the Primary Insight is one with its Existence, it follows that the Primary Insight is also the Primary Being.

Consequently the following conclusions are clear:

If the Primary Insight is one, and the Primary Insight is the Primary Being, then the Primary Being is one.

If the Primary Insight is simple, and the Primary Insight is the Primary Being, then the Primary Being is simple.

If the Primary Insight is independent, and the Primary Insight is the Primary Being, then the Primary Being is independent.

If the Primary Insight is perfect, and the Primary Insight is the Primary Being, then the Primary Being is perfect.

If the Primary Insight is unlimited, and the Primary Insight is the Primary Being, then the Primary Being is infinite, for the infinite is the unlimited.

If the Primary Insight is spiritual, and the Primary Insight is the Primary Being, then the Primary Being is spiritual.

If the Primary Insight is timeless, and the Primary Insight is the Primary Being, then the Primary Being is eternal, for the eternal is the timeless.

If the Primary Insight is self-explanatory, and the Primary Insight is the Primary Being, then the Primary Being is self-explanatory.

Further, the Primary Being is also necessary being, because its very essence is to exist.

The Primary Being is not an accident, because accidents are not necessary; and again, because accidents are dependent on substance, and the Primary Being is independent, as already seen.

But the Primary Being is substance. For the characteristic notes of substance are unity and independence. But the Primary Being is one and independent. Therefore the Primary Being is spiritual substance. But the Primary Being is unlike other substance, in that it supports no accidents.

It has been denied that the Primary Being is an accident, or that the Primary Substance has accidents. But it may be asked, does the Primary Being have characteristics? For example, the Primary Being was equated with spiritual substance. Is "spiritual" a characteristic of the Primary Substance? To answer this question, a brief excursus on analogical language will be necessary.

It should be noticed, first of all, that the Primary Insight is not understood directly. Were a human person to understand the Primary Insight directly, that person would *be* the Primary Insight, because in the Primary Insight, as already seen, there can be no distinction of understanding and understood. Therefore the Primary Insight is understood only indirectly. Being was understood by an extrapolation from the structure of knowing; it was indirectly defined as the object of the pure desire to know. The Primary Insight was a further extrapolation, indirectly defined as the insight adequate to being. Such indirect speech is usually termed *analogical*. It refers to the Primary Insight by using words which mean something the same, and something different, than they mean in ordinary usage.

Thus an Unlimited Insight is somewhat similar, and somewhat dissimilar, from an ordinary insight. It has something in common, because the ordinary insight is an act of understanding, and the Unlimited Insight is an act of understanding. At the same time, the acts of understanding are quite different, because one is limited, and the other unlimited; the first is but a pale reflection of the second.

Similarly, the Primary Substance and other substances are similar in that they are one, and independent; but they are different in that the Primary Substance supports no accidents.

So a characteristic may be predicated of the Primary Insight. For example, it may be said that the Primary Insight is wise. For wisdom is a certain perfection of knowing, and the Primary Insight is perfect knowing. Yet *wise* is not predicated of the Primary Substance as an accident of a substance, for the Primary Substance has no accidents. What is actually being predicated is not an accident *wise* but a substantial Wisdom. Further, that Wisdom is not other than the Primary Insight itself, for the Primary Insight is simple. And a similar analysis can be made of any other characteristic predicated of the Primary Substance.

The Primary Being is good. If the cosmic account of the good presented in the last chapter is correct, then the good is convertible with the intelligible. But the Primary Being is perfectly intelligible, because it is one with the Primary Insight and the Primary Intelligible. Therefore, the Primary Being is perfectly good. Further, according to the preceding analysis of analogical language, the Primary Being is substantial Goodness; and that Goodness is not other than the Being. Thus the Primary Being is also the Primary Good.

The Primary Being is also perfectly loving. For to will, to choose, and to love are spiritual goods. If the Primary Being were not perfectly loving, it would not be perfectly good.

As is clear, a similar argument could be made regarding any spiritual good. But this permits a further clarification of analogical language. For what is true of spiritual goods is not true of physical goods. For example, it may be good for a human being to be tall. But one cannot argue, the Primary Insight must be tall, because otherwise it would not be perfectly good. "To be tall" presumes having a body; and the Primary Insight has no body. When physical perfections are applied to the Primary Insight, consequently, they are not applied analogically, but metaphorically. When Genesis, for example, says that God walked in the garden in the cool of the evening, it is using metaphorical language. What Ambrose was assuring Augustine was that such metaphorical language did not detract from the spirituality of God.

The Primary Being is also omnipotent. For if the Primary Being could not effect all the reflections of itself that the Primary Insight understands as possible, then the Primary Being would be deficient in goodness.

The Primary Being is therefore the First Cause. For any other intelligibles are understood by the Primary Insight and willed by omnipotent being.

The Primary Being is accordingly the Creator, bringing into being and sustaining in existence any other instances of the intelligible and the good.

But the one, simple, infinite, eternal, omniscient, and omnipotent spiritual substance which is the knowing and loving cause of all things is what is traditionally known as God.

29

The Existence of God

The last chapter has formulated the idea of God, beginning with the results of the inward journey. Now the question for reflection arises, Does God exist? At the end of chapter 27 it was suggested that the desire to know should be as wide as being: no question should be arbitrarily brushed aside. Above all, this question is not to be arbitrarily brushed aside, because it so deeply affects the way a person views the universe.

At first sight, it may appear simple to show that God exists. For God is Necessary Being. But Necessary Being must exist. Therefore God must exist.

Again, in the Primary Insight essence is one with existence. Thus it is the very nature of the Primary Insight to exist. It would be unnatural for the Primary Insight not to exist. Therefore God must exist.

Again, God is Perfect Being. But an existent God is obviously more perfect than a non-existent God. Therefore God must exist.

This last may be recognized as somewhat similar to Anselm's ontological argument: God is that than which nothing greater can be conceived. But if God does not exist, then something greater can be conceived. Therefore God must exist.

Descartes has an interesting variation on this argument: The idea of God is an infinite idea. But a human being has a finite mind. A finite mind cannot produce an infinite idea. We find in our minds, however, the infinite idea. But that must mean that God has placed it there. Therefore God must exist.

The problem with the above arguments is that—as will be remembered—the preceding chapter began with a postulation. A postulate occurs on the level of understanding. So, before drawing any conclusions from the results of that postulate, one must ask a prior question: Is the postulate true? If the insight adequate to being exists, then God must exist. But first one must establish whether the insight adequate to being exists. Clearly, any argument for the existence of God from the idea of God, bypassing the question for reflection, is invalid.

If the human being grasped the unlimited insight directly, then the existence of God would be self-evident: for the unlimited insight answers all questions for reflection, and understands the evidence for its own existence. But, as already mentioned, the human being who would grasp the unlimited insight directly would have to *be* the unlimited insight. As it is, the human being grasps the unlimited insight only indirectly, by analogy, by an extrapolation.

Thus Descartes's premise must be met with a distinction: the human being possesses a finite idea of the infinite. The idea is of the infinite, for the desire to know strains and stretches beyond any fixed limits to the unlimited, the infinite. Yet the idea itself remains finite because, as Descartes correctly saw, a finite mind cannot produce an infinite idea.

Again the influence of cognitional theory is significant here. If one holds with Descartes that the criterion of truth is the clear and distinct idea, then the clear and distinct idea of God implies the existence of God. But if one holds to the results of the inner journey as traced in the preceding pages, then truth is found in the judgment, and the idea, however clear and distinct, must still face the question for reflection.

Yet this much must be conceded to Anselm and Descartes: the idea of the infinite is indeed the grandest idea the human mind has ever elaborated. Than that nothing greater can be conceived.

If one cannot argue to the existence of God from the Primary Intelligible, the idea of the infinite, then the argument must begin with other intelligibles, that is, with creatures. In Kantian language, the argument for God's existence cannot be a priori, and so it must be a posteriori. That seems to be in keeping with the Scriptures, which teach that God can be known through his creatures, and suggest that this represents the native power of the human mind. "For all men were by nature foolish who were in ignorance of God, and who from the good things seen did not succeed in knowing him who is, and from studying the works did not discern the artisan. . . . For from the greatness and the beauty of created things their original author, by analogy, is seen" (Wis 13:1, 5). "In fact, whatever can be known about God is clear to them; he himself made it so. Since the creation of the world, invisible realities, God's eternal power and divinity, have become visible, recognized through the things he has made" (Rom 1:19-20).

Thomas Aquinas presents five arguments for the existence of God in the *Summa Theologiae*. The first is from change in creatures to their unchanged cause; the second is from created effects to the first cause. The third argues from contingent being to necessary being. The fourth begins with created grades of perfection and rises to the most excellent and perfect being. The fifth argues from purpose and design in nature to its Universal Intender. Lonergan, in chapter 19 of *Insight*, offers one demanding and challenging proof which formulates the basic principle of all the Thomistic proofs.

The reader is referred to those sources for a rigorous presentation. Here the scope will be more modest: first, to suggest that there are only two logical possibilities:

> Either God exists, or
> God does not exist.

Second,

> If God exists, then the universe is intelligible;
> If God does not exist, then the universe is unintelligible.

Before proceeding further, let the universe be defined as the sum of all intelligibles other than the Primary Intelligible.

The first alternative, then, is that the universe is intelligible, that it makes sense. The second alternative is that the universe is unintelligible, absurd. To put it in other terms, the question, What is the meaning of the universe? is answered with a direct insight in the first alternative, but it must be met with an inverse insight in the second: the question is illegitimate, for there is nothing here to be understood.

The goal of science, as formulated previously, is the complete explanation of all physical phenomena. Hence it would make no sense for scientists, asked about the reason or cause of any phenomenon, to answer, "There is no cause." For example, if scientists are asked, "Why is the sky blue?" they cannot answer, in the scientific spirit, "There's no reason; it's just blue." They may well say, "We don't have a complete answer for that yet; we're still investigating it; that's an open question in present-day science"; but they cannot simply say, "That has no answer; don't ask!"

That spirit of open inquiry has only to be widened to the universe as a whole. "What is the cause of the universe? What is the reason it exists?" On the first alternative, the answer is, "God is the cause of the universe. For in every being other than God, form can be distinguished from existence. So finite being does not necessarily exist; it just happens to exist. Thus finite being is not self-explanatory; it must have an explanation outside itself. That explanation can only be God, the necessary and self-explanatory being."

On the second alternative, the answer must be, "There is no reason. The universe just exists. There is no cause, and the question makes no sense; don't ask!"

Jean-Paul Sartre must be credited with exploring thoroughly and rigorously the logic of the second alternative. As he realized with perfect accuracy, if God does not exist, then the universe is absurd.

The same alternatives are discovered by asking, "What is the purpose of the universe? What is the universe for?" On the first alternative, the answer is God. As the human being is oriented to the good, so all creatures, on their own level, and according to their own nature, are oriented to the good; and that good is ultimately the unlimited good, God.

On the second alternative, the answer must be that the universe is for nothing. It has no end, no purpose. One might say that other creatures are for the human being, the high point of the cosmos. But what is the human being for? For others, one might answer; for the community, the more socially minded might answer; for the state, the socialist may say. But what are other human beings, or the human community, or the state for? Ultimately, one must say, for nothing. Again Sartre had it right: If God does not exist, the human being is a useless passion.

Though no rigorous proof has been offered, the reader is left, perhaps uncomfortably, with some stark alternatives. Do I brush these questions aside arbitrarily, or do I face them head-on? Can I find some way between an existent God and an intelligible universe, and a non-existent God and an absurd universe, or not? If not, do I opt for the absurd universe? Or do I affirm the existence of God? And if I do, what implications does that have for my living?

The last question suggests that the question of morality needs now to be re-thought in the light of God. If God exists, then the unlimited good the will so insatiably seeks turns out to be none other than the unlimited good, God. Further, the native desire for the good is no accident, but is implanted in the human being by the Creator, God. Consequently, a person who violates that desire for the good by doing something unreasonable and unintelligent is violating, not only the native desire for good, but also the design of God. Therefore moral failure is not only a departure from the in-built moral compass intending the good, it is sin against God.

On the other hand, if God does not exist, if the universe is absurd, and the human being is a useless passion, then one might well question why any one course of action is to be preferred to any other. What ultimate difference does it make?

In these pages the technique of performative contradiction has often been employed, and it may again find an application here. The drive to know is a drive for intelligibility. To affirm the existence of God is coherent with that drive, for God is the Intelligibility of the universe, the cause, reason, and explanation of all those intelligibles which do not explain themselves. To deny the existence of God is to be incoherent, for the desire for intelligibility would be positing a final unintelligibility in the universe. Still, one might well ask, If the universe is absurd, what is the point of being coherent?

30

A Final Wisdom

Chapter 9 considered the relationship of common sense and science, and noted the hostility and mutual suspicion that often characterize the relation of the person of common sense and the scientist. The chapter ended with a plea to recognize that both kinds of knowing were fully human, but it left unanswered some further questions: Is there any knowledge that mediates the conflict of common sense and science? Or is the human mind doomed ever to be at odds with itself? The answer to this question will proceed in two stages: the need for a wisdom, and the proposal of a wisdom.

The Need for a Wisdom

The person who lives by common-sense knowledge often thinks that knowledge all-sufficient. The milkmaids who saw Thales fall into a well had no interest in gazing at the stars, and Martha wondered what Mary was doing, sitting and talking, while there was work to be done. Goodyear's wife, as well, must sometimes have scratched her head to know what her husband was on about. But a little reflection shows that common sense cannot be the final form of human knowledge.

The first argument is historical. Were common-sense knowledge all-sufficient, then the theoretical questions of Socrates, and the Greek breakthrough to science, would never have occurred. Consequently none of the deliverances of modern science would be available. Science is a withdrawal from short-term practicality, yet often it returns with products that are eminently practical—like rubber tires. The strange paradox is that practicality, focused as it is on the short-term, ultimately becomes impractical; and that the scientist, who deserts short-term practicality to explore theoretical questions, is at least sometimes being altogether practical. In some cases the time gap is very large. The Greeks worked out the theory of the parabola hundreds of years before Christ; it was turned to practical use only in the early modern period, when it became necessary to calculate the trajectory of a cannon-ball. For the person of short-term practicality, something two thousand years away is utterly irrelevant; but the consequence is that short-term practicality is blind to long-term consequences.

The second argument delves deeper than considerations of practicality. The all-sufficiency of common-sense knowledge deprives the human mind of its full development. The person of common sense understands to live, so that intelligence is always harnessed to practical ends. Only the Greek breakthrough freed the mind from its traces and bridle to explore its own inner thrust—which has been seen to be unlimited. The restriction to short-term practicality simply rules out all such development.

Common-sense knowing, then, cannot be the final form of human knowledge, because it arbitrarily brushes aside all theoretical questions. It fails to be open to the full scope of being.

What about science? Can it be the final form of knowing? Science is usually understood first of all in terms of the physical sciences: physics, chemistry, biology, and so on. As seen already, their goal is the full exploration of all physical phenomena. But here appears already their crucial lack: they are concerned with bodies, not with spirit. The exclusion of spirit is also the exclusion of active intelligence. It should be obvious that a science that excludes intelligence from its purview is not a good candidate for adjudicating the conflict between common sense and science.

What about the human sciences? The Germans call them the *Geisteswissenschaften*, the "spiritual sciences": psychology, sociology, anthropology, linguistics, semiotics, and so on. One problem with these sciences, at least in their present forms, is that they claim to be "value-free." But human living, as chapter 26 showed, is inescapably involved with values. Therefore a value-free science cannot be the final form of human knowing. Indeed, that is often the problem of the contemporary world, in which the physical and the human sciences reveal possibilities without being able to say whether they are good or not; technical possibility becomes the law of action, from atom bombs and gene manipulation to brainwashing and psychological torture.

What about the inner science proposed in chapter 21? It would appear to be adequate to the task of conciliating common sense and outer science, because it grasps their common root in cognitional process. It understands both what they have in common (the structure of knowing) and what sets them apart (common sense understands to live, while theoretical reason lives to understand).

This proposal brings into focus the deeper limitations of science as a final form of knowing. Science, by its nature, moves from the particular to the general. The move to the concept, as seen already, is a great boon to human knowing, because it is a short-cut to knowing all substances of the same type. But a price is also paid, because the universal abstracts from the particular. Human life, however, is lived in the particular, in the realm of common sense. (Jung reflected that his autobiography could not be scientific, because science considers the general, not the particular.) The morality derivable from the structure of knowing had to remain general. But actual moral choices are between particular courses of action, to be performed by a particular person, in a particular situation.

Further, science is generally wedded, to a greater or lesser degree, to logic. Aristotle saw science as a deductive expansion from a small number of primary premises, akin to Euclid's geometry. The realm of science is that of the universal and the necessary. Even in modern science, which stresses more what happens to be rather than what has to be, definitions, logical deductions, and conclusions are highly prized.

Logical knowing, however, cannot be the final form of human knowing, and that has been grasped in both the ancient and the modern worlds. Aristotle came to it this way: Logic proceeds by syllogism. But each syllogism needs two premises to generate one conclusion. If those two premises are to be logically demonstrated, they will require four premises; and those four, eight prior premises; and those eight, sixteen; and so on. In short, scientific and logical knowing cannot ground itself. Beyond science, Aristotle held, there must be *nous*, an intuitive knowledge of self-evident first principles, and wisdom.

That same conclusion finds notable corroboration in the twentieth century in the work of Kurt Gödel. He showed that in any closed logical system, a question may be asked that cannot be answered within that system. Any set of premises can be shown to generate problems which require, for their solution, an additional premise, and so a larger logical system. The same will be true of that larger system, and so on. The upshot is that no logical system can ground itself.

In sum, no science—whether physical science, human science, or inner science—can be the final form of human knowing. That role must rather be fulfilled by a wisdom which is able to grasp at once the general and the particular, the factual and the valuable, the logical and what escapes logic.

Proposal of a Wisdom

The metaphor of a journey from darkness into light was seen in the first chapter to be appropriate to three great turning points in human history: the Greek breakthrough to science, the Christian experience of the Light of the world, and the modern Enlightenment. The proposal here is that a final wisdom is best fashioned by gathering the best, all that is good and positive, from these three great enlightenments.

The first such element is the Greek discovery of the mind. In the leisure of the Greek city-state civilization the human mind first took control of itself, set its own agenda, and established order in its own house. In this Greek breakthrough lay the beginnings of definition, logic, and science. What is notable is that this was a discovery, once for all, not just for Greece, but for the human race. Wherever in the world today definition is exploited, logic is employed, or science is utilized, a direct debt is owed to Greece. No one before had discovered these ideas and techniques, and everyone since has learned them, ultimately, from the Greeks.

One drawback of Greek thought was that it overly stressed the necessary. Science was limited to the universal and the necessary. Modern science, on the other hand, has discovered itself to be the study not of what has to be, but of what happens to be.

Another lack in the Greek breakthrough is an inadequate idea of God. In Plato the highest reality is the Idea of the Good; yet that remains mysterious—almost always, it seems, beyond direct or clear statement. Aristotle has a clearer idea: the Self-thinking Thought. Yet this idea too is deficient: there is no will, no love, no concern, and no providence for creatures.

The Christian breakthrough also exhibits a number of strengths. One is its strong stress on the primacy of the spiritual. As Jesus said, "Do not fear those who deprive the body of life but cannot destroy the soul. Rather, fear him who can destroy both body and soul in Gehenna" (Matt 10:28). Another is that the ultimate knowing is placed not in reason, but in faith. Beyond the knowledge of reason is the enlightenment of God's own wisdom. "There is, to be sure, a certain wisdom which we express among the spiritually mature. It is not a wisdom of this age, however. . . . No, what we utter is God's wisdom, a mysterious, a hidden wisdom" (1 Cor 2:6-7).

For Samuel Beckett, man is waiting for Godot, who may or may not exist, may or may not be coming. But the Christian good news is not only that God exists—a truth knowable to human reason—but that he comes, bringing a divine wisdom and a divine love to human affairs.

Christianity integrated into itself the Greek wisdom. The patristic era especially took on the thought of Plato. A common bond was found in *logos* (literally, "word," but in Greek carrying the wider meaning of "reason, rationality, order, intelligibility"). On the one hand, it was the Logos who came personally in Christianity. As John's Gospel begins, "In the beginning was the Logos, and the Logos was with God, and the Logos was God" (1:1). On the other hand, logos was central to Greek thought, as the very underlying order and rationality of the world. In practically his last words to his friends, Socrates warns in the *Phaedo* of the danger of becoming "misologists," haters of reason. And this in spite of the fact that Socrates was in prison for his devotion to reason. He could well have escaped the executioner, but he challenged his friends to show him that it would be the reasonable thing to do, and they failed. Thus Socrates lived and died the intellectual morality of never affirming without sufficient evidence, and the larger morality of doing nothing unreasonable.

If the notion of logos formed the bridge between Christian and Platonic wisdom in the patristic age, the High Middle Ages saw Christianity absorb Aristotle as well, especially in the thought of Thomas Aquinas.

This marriage of Jerusalem and Athens may be seen, in retrospect, as a mating of strength with strength. The Jewish and early Christian weakness in systematic thought is corrected by absorbing the fruits of the Greek breakthrough. On the other hand, the abstractness of Greek thought is anchored by the concreteness of the incarnation, the overemphasis on necessity is tempered by the "scandal of particularity," and reason shelters under the canopy of faith. The overly intellectual nature of Aristotle's God is met by the Jewish and Christian God, a strong-willed God of love. In one passage in Ephesians Paul piles up words referring to the will of God: "In him we were chosen; for in the decree of God, who administers everything according to his will and counsel, we were predestined to praise his glory" (1:5-6).

The drawback of Christianity is its tendency to fission. In the fourth century the Arians were excluded, in the fifth century the Nestorians and the Monophysites. The ninth to eleventh centuries saw the split of the Eastern and Western Churches, and the sixteenth century the division of Catholic and Protestant. The history of subsequent Protestantism is largely the history of further fissioning.

Such internal division is not the ideal of Christianity itself. Indeed, on the night before he died Christ prayed for the unity of his Church, linking it with his own unity with the Father: "I pray also for those who will believe in me . . . that all may be one as you, Father, are in me, and I in you" (John 17:20-21). In the very same discourse, he offered a new commandment: "I give you a new commandment: Love one another. Such as my love has been for you, so must your love be for each other. This is how all will know you for my disciples: your love for one another" (John 15:12, 8).

Nevertheless, as it has been lived out historically, Christianity has been full of division. It was precisely a despair over the hundred years of war between Protestants and Catholics that led to the modern Enlightenment.

What is positive about that Enlightenment, then, is its goal of finding a way for people to live together in tolerance and civil peace, whatever their conflicting religious beliefs.

The Enlightenment is also notable for its sponsorship of modern science. Science was invented by the Greeks, but the modern age found a new way to correct the Greek obsession with necessity. Galileo, as seen earlier, put a new stress on observation and measurement. Emphasis shifted from what had to be to what happened to be. Nevertheless, ironically, it took a long time for scientific theory to catch up with scientific practice. Descartes, Newton, and Kant all still thought in terms of Aristotelian science. It was only the discovery of alternative geometries in the nineteenth century, and of relativity and the Heisenberg uncertainty principle in the twentieth, that led to the final abandonment, in theory as well as in practice, of Aristotelian necessity.

A third positive strength of the Enlightenment was its robust confidence in reason. It affirmed the world to be intelligible and set out, with the tools of logic and modern science, to discover its order.

Unfortunately, the third Enlightenment did not mesh as smoothly with the second as the second did with the first. In fact, the modern Enlightenment began by appealing to the first against the second. It appealed to Greek and Roman civilization as an arsenal and a standpoint from which to attack Christianity. That is what is most negative about the modern Enlightenment: its hostility to the Christian enlightenment.

A second problem with the Enlightenment is that it overstresses the logical. Descartes wanted to found a logical system on the unassailable ground of the Cogito. In doing so, he was unaware of the truth already discovered by Aristotle, and to be re-discovered by Gödel: no logical system can ground itself. In a larger sense, the Enlightenment as a whole makes the same mistake: when it rejects faith to build a world on reason, it does not realize that reason is ultimately powerless to ground itself. In cutting itself off from Christianity—however understandable such a move may have been historically—it also destroyed its own roots.

As an historical experiment, the robust confidence in reason does not sustain itself. Its tragic trajectory can be traced from Descartes, who dreamed of a new and more rigorously logical philosophy, to Sartre, who declared the universe absurd, leaving reason little scope but to document its own uselessness.

The late nineteenth century evinces a wonderful paradox in this connection. The Enlightenment had begun by accusing Christianity of childishness, superstition, obscurity. It would appeal to reason for a clearing up of these medieval obscurancies. Yet reason gradually lost its self-confidence. Already Kant decreed that metaphysics is impossible, that God and even the self are, strictly speaking, unknowable. In the late nineteenth century Friedrich Nietzsche proclaimed the death of God; Sartre cannot be far behind. Yet against this very background the First Vatican Council defined that reason, by its natural powers, is able to know the existence of God.

The proposal here is to accept all that is positive about the modern Enlightenment, but to reject its rejection of the amalgam of Greek, Jewish, and Christian wisdom.

The personal journey fittingly ends here. For if there is anything that is personal, it is the embracing of a final wisdom. A wisdom can only be proposed. It cannot, by its nature, be demonstrated, for wisdom escapes and goes beyond the logical.

Envoi: Two

The last chapter spoke of a journey ending, but that is not quite accurate. A book may end; but the personal journey goes on. Many questions regarding cognitional activity were strewn by the wayside in the above pages; they remain to be answered. The moral implications of the inward journey were hardly touched on in chapter 26; chapters 28 and 29 only grazed the question of God; and chapter 30 did no more than refer to his possible intervention in human history. All these questions, and many, many more, may be pursued in Lonergan's *Insight*, for which this work is intended merely as a propadeutic. Truly, there is journey enough here to last a lifetime.

In closing, one last consideration may be given to Plato's myth of the cave. In the gradual habituation of the inner sight, first to shadows, then reflections, then things themselves, then the night sky, the ultimate vision is that of the sun.

> And so, finally, I suppose he would be able to look upon the sun itself and see its true nature, not by reflections in water or phantasms of it in an alien setting, but in and by itself in its own place. . . .
>
> And at this point he would infer and conclude that this it is that provides the seasons and the courses of the year and presides over all things in the visible region, and is in some sort the cause of all these things that they had seen (748–749).

At the risk of reading too much into the text, Plato appears to be using the sun here as a metaphor for God—or, as he would probably prefer to phrase it, the Idea of the Good. The whole myth is a metaphor for the intellectual journey. The sun is the last and highest object to be seen in this journey. Obviously, this is not the physical sun, but the ultimate in the intelligible sphere. And what could that be, but the Primary Intelligible, the Idea of the Good, or God? And Plato further suggests this, because the metaphorical sun has the characteristics of the Creator: "This it is that provides the seasons and the courses of the year and presides over all things in the visible region, and is in some sort the cause of all these things that they had seen."

Thus Plato suggests the ultimate significance of the inner journey: it may lead to an encounter with God.

At the beginning it was pointed out that the inner journey was both arduous and momentous. At the time that may have seemed hyperbole, the exaggeration of a writer overly impressed with what he had to say, or a disciple unduly smitten with the brilliance of Lonergan's thought. But in the light of the last interpretation of the myth of the cave, there may be reason to soften that judgment. The arduous nature of the journey has, in all likelihood, been amply verified; and if the inner journey leads to a vision of God, then it is momentous indeed.

Perhaps the most appropriate farewell from author to reader, then, is taken from contemporary Spanish: "Vaya con Dios." "Go with God." There is a similar English farewell; though not much used today, it remains part of our tradition: "Godspeed on the journey!"

Works Cited

Boswell, James. *The Life of Samuel Johnson* in *Great Books of the Western World*, vol. 44. Chicago: William Benton, 1952.

The Collected Dialogues of Plato, eds. Edith Hamilton and Huntington Cairns, trans. Paul Shorey. Princeton: Princeton University Press, 1969.

Doyle, Arthur Conan. *The Complete Sherlock Holmes.* Garden City, N.Y.: Doubleday, 1930.

Kant, Immanuel. *Critique of Pure Reason*, trans. Norman Kemp Smith. New York: St. Martin's, 1963.

Lonergan, Bernard J. F. *A Second Collection.* Philadelphia: Westminster, 1974.

The Philosophical Works of Descartes. Trans. Elizabeth S. Haldane and G.R.T. Ross. Vol. 1. Cambridge, England: University Press, 1968.

St. Augustine, *Confessions*, trans. Vernon J. Bourke, *The Fathers of the Church*, vol. 21. New York: Fathers of the Church, 1953.

St. Thomas Aquinas: Summa theologiae, ed. T. Gilby. 61vv. London: Eyre and Spottiswoode, 1964–1980.

Index of Proper Names